Independent Essays

INDEPENDENT ESSAYS

by

JOHN SPARROW

GREENWOOD PRESS, PUBLISHERS
WESTPORT, CONNECTICUT

Library of Congress Cataloging in Publication Data

Sparrow, John Hanbury Angus, 1906-
    Independent essays.

    Reprint of the 1963 ed. published by Faber and Faber,
London.
    Includes bibliographical references.
    1. English literature--History and criticism--Ad-
dresses, essays, lectures. 2. Poetry--Addresses,
essays, lectures. I. Title.
[PR99.S58 1977]   820'.9   76-49841
ISBN 0-8371-9361-3

820.9
S737ū

Originally published in 1963 by Faber and Faber, London

Reprinted with the permission of Faber & Faber Ltd.

Reprinted in 1977 by Greenwood Press, Inc.

Library of Congress Catalog Card Number   76-49841

ISBN 0-8371-9361-3

Printed in the United States of America

To my old friend
ROY HARROD
in admiration

Acknowledgments

GREAT POETRY, a Warton Lecture delivered to the British Academy, appeared originally in the Academy's *Proceedings*. IN MEMORIAM was written as an introduction to the Nonesuch Press edition of that poem and THE POETRY OF JOHN BETJEMAN is based on the preface to SELECTED POEMS (John Murray, 1948). BARRIE AND HIMSELF first appeared in *The Spectator*. All the other essays in this book are reprinted from *The Times Literary Supplement*.

Contents

Foreword

If there is anything that makes the essays in this collection worth preserving it is, I think, the attitude suggested by its title: in each of them I have taken a book or a subject presenting itself for review (and most of them were 'reviews' in the technical sense of the word) and have tried to think out for myself its implications or to assess its qualities without yielding to any pressure from traditional or contemporary fashions in thought or taste. They might also perhaps be called 'independent essays' in another sense, in that they are independent of each other, and do not give expression to any coherent critical doctrine or reveal any consistent attitude on fundamental questions that seem to trouble many of those who write about literature today. To this, I can only answer that that is the way my mind works: abstractions and generalizations do not come easily to me; I am not tempted to theorize about the writer's position in society, or the possibility of writing poetry in the twentieth century, or the reflection of the contemporary consciousness in the novel, or a dozen other concepts which too often, when I read criticism, seem to me to obscure rather than to illumine the page. Such phrases, of course, though critics do not always make it clear exactly what they have in mind when they use them, are not unmeaning, and something useful can be said about the things they stand for—but it will not, I am afraid, be said by me. Instead, what I have to offer is simply a personal judgment on a number of works and topics that seemed to me to be worth the attention of the reflective reader.

J.S.

Great Poetry[1]

What do we mean when we talk—as we so often and so glibly do—about 'great literature' or 'great art', about 'a great painter' or 'a great poet'?

Most people, when they use the word 'great' in such a context, probably have at the back of their minds a vague conception of outstanding and established excellence—eminence based on superior achievement and attested by the authority of acknowledged experts. That is the common reader's idea of greatness, and in that sense the word is often used by publishers with a popular market in view: *Great Poems by Great Poets* was a favourite volume with me when I was not of an age to be troubled by the problems lurking in its title.

People who use the word in this sense take much for granted, at any rate when they apply it to the artist. Clearly they have in mind something more than popularity or long-standing reputation; they presuppose some quality, some real merit, in the artist or his work; but what that quality may be is a question they are content to leave to others. And in this they are wise, for artistic merit is not merely an indeterminate concept, like being tall (for instance) or being old; it is a concept involving questions that are difficult, some would say impossible, to answer. Though we might not all agree about the point of height or age at which an author should be called tall or old, we all know what we mean by height and age, and agree about how they should be measured. But there is no such universal agreement about how to measure artistic or literary excellence, or even about what it is.

Certainly we often use the word in this sense, superficial though its use may be, in ordinary conversation, and not only when it is

[1] The Warton Lecture on English Poetry, British Academy, 1960.

[13]

about artists that we are talking.[1] You can be, in this sense, a great craftsman or a great cricketer, just as you can be a great creative artist—Sheraton was great in this sense as well as Shakespeare, Bradman as well as Beethoven; you can be, in this sense, a great general or a great judge.[2]

But often when we speak of a great poet or artist we have in mind something different from the popular conception. Shakespeare and Donne, Milton and Gray, Shelley and Keats, Byron and Wordsworth, Tennyson and Browning—all of these are certainly great poets in the popular sense, just as Jane Austen and Scott and Dickens and Trollope and Tolstoy and Meredith are, in that sense, all great novelists. But even the common reader will feel that there is a·distinction to be made between them, and in this very matter of greatness. If pressed, he would probably describe it as merely a difference of degree: he might say that Tolstoy is a 'greater' novelist than Trollope, and Wordsworth a 'greater' poet than Gray. And if he felt uneasily aware that this was not a full statement of the case, he might express what he felt by saying that Tolstoy and Wordsworth were 'really' or 'truly' great, while Trollope and Gray were not—thus admitting that the difference was not merely in degree, but in kind.

If we want to know what constitutes 'true' greatness in literature we shall have to go elsewhere than to the common reader. At this point it is likely that words will fail him—and not him alone. For

[1] The word was very frequently used, often in the superlative, in the recent trial concerning D. H. Lawrence's *Lady Chatterley's Lover*. One witness, for instance, said, 'I would say he is certainly among the six greatest, the five or six greatest, writers in English literature in this century. . . . I wouldn't rank the book among the greatest of the works he wrote, although I think certain passages of it are among the greatest things that he wrote. . . . I would say the expurgated passages come into this class.' Another declared, 'He seemed to me then, and seems to me now, one of the greatest writers in a decade of giants. He made a great difference to me, and I owe a great debt to him.' I suppose it was in the popular sense, in so far as they had any clear idea of what they meant by it, that these experts used the word.

[2] It is not in all fields of activity that greatness is attainable, even in this popular, superficial sense; it can be achieved by the racing motorist but not by the taxi-driver, by the captain of industry but not by the errand-boy. The criterion would seem to be not the scope for originality, but rather the opportunity for exercising unusual gifts or extraordinary skill.

while it is easy to provide a description adequate for everyday purposes of what is meant by greatness in its popular sense, about 'true'
greatness it is very difficult to say, usefully or helpfully, anything at
all. Listen to the opening sentences of William Michael Rossetti's
preface to his edition of Shelley's *Poetical Works*:

'Chaucer, Shakespeare, Milton, Shelley—these are, I believe, the
four sublimest sons of song that England has to boast of among the
mighty dead—say rather among the undying, the never-to-die. Let
us remember also two exceptional phenomena, an "inspired plough-
man", Burns, and an unparalleled poetess, Mrs. Browning, and be
thankful for such a national destiny. There are plenty of others: but
those four are, if I mistake not, *the* four.'

Well, you may say, that is only a fresh proof of what we have
always known—that William Michael Rossetti, for all his love of
poetry, was not to be taken seriously as a critic. Listen, then, to one
who has a better claim to be accounted a critic than William Michael
Rossetti; listen to Swinburne:

'The great man of whom I am about to speak seems to me a figure
more utterly companionless, more incomparable with others, than
any of his kind—'

—so Swinburne opens the essay prefixed to his Selection from
Coleridge; and he goes on:

'In all times there have been gods that alighted and giants that
appeared on earth; the ranks of great men are properly divisible, not
into thinkers and workers, but into Titans and Olympians. Sometimes a supreme poet is both at once: such above all men is Aeschy-
lus; so also Dante, Michael Angelo, Shakespeare, Milton, Goethe,
Hugo are gods at once and giants; they have the lightning as well as
the light of the world, and in hell they have command as in heaven;
they can see in the night as by day. As godlike as these, even as the
divinest of them, a poet such as Coleridge needs not the thews and
organs of any Titan to make him greater.'

Plainly the idea of greatness that Swinburne had in mind when he
wrote those words was something different from the popular idea,
from mere 'eminence' or the literary excellence on which such
eminence is founded.

But what it is—what qualities, gifts, attributes, he was thinking of

[15]

—Swinburne does not make clear. He is, as it were, struck dumb; the word 'great' in his mouth is little more than an exclamation mark; he can only gasp his admiration. Indeed, he himself confesses that this is so:

'Of his flight and his song when in the fit element [he says, of *Christabel* and *The Ancient Mariner*] it is hard to speak at all, hopeless to speak adequately. It is natural that there should be nothing like them discoverable in any human work, natural that his poetry at its highest should be, as it is, beyond all praise and all words of men. . . . When it has been said that such melodies were never heard, such dreams never dreamed, such speech never spoken, the chief thing remains unsaid, and unspeakable. There is a charm upon these poems which can only be felt in silent submission of wonder.'

It is easy to smile at this—hard, perhaps, not to smile at it. One is tempted to say that Swinburne would have done better to yield completely to the 'silent submission of wonder'. But that would not be altogether fair. For Swinburne feels very strongly about Coleridge, and he wants his readers to know this and to feel as he does, and that aim is not an unworthy one. If he trusts too much to the infectiousness of enthusiasm, we should remember that in the criticism of art, reasoned praise is always more difficult than reasoned blame—it is harder to explain why you like something than to explain why you dislike it. And explanation in this case was peculiarly difficult because the conception that Swinburne was trying to communicate—the 'greatness' of a poet or his work—is not an easy conception to identify.

Hard it may be, but Swinburne never even makes the attempt; he is content to pour out a stream of phrases that tell us really no more than that Coleridge's poetry affected him very deeply; and to be content with this is to abdicate the position of critic. If Swinburne had supposed that *Kubla Khan* acted on him in the same sort of way as the opium that produced it acted on Coleridge, then we should have no right to complain that he has treated us only to an account of his reactions to it; but he evidently believed that his reactions were directly and recognizably related to some actual superiority in Coleridge's poems, and we therefore have a right to ask him to give us some idea of what he thinks that that superiority consists in. It is not

[16]

the critic's business to explain *why* we should react as we do to the qualities present in a work of art—that, perhaps, cannot be done even by the psychologist—but to detect those qualities, to distinguish between them, to disengage and unfold them, as it were, and exhibit them for the inspection of the reader—this, surely, is an essential task of criticism. And this is something that Swinburne entirely fails to do.

Now, for myself, when the writers I have already mentioned present themselves to my mind, I find that, like the common reader, I naturally think of some of them as being 'great' in a sense in which others of them are not: Tolstoy, but not Trollope; Wordsworth, but not Gray. And while it is difficult to say just what this 'greatness' is, it is plain that it is not simply a matter of literary excellence, whatever literary excellence may be. Still less does it depend upon what class of literature their works belong to—a novelist can be great in this sense as well as a poet; a lyrical poet as well as the writer of an epic.

Now if I am not to be relegated, with Swinburne and William Michael Rossetti, to the class of the merely enraptured, I must give some account of why I should feel this; of what it is in a poet that impels me to call him great.

In trying to answer this question, I do not begin, or hope to end, with a definition either of greatness or of poetry itself. Critics have defined poetry in many ways, and prescribed various aims for poets: the poet's aim is self-expression; the poet's aim is communication; poetry is making; poetry is play; poetry is an essence; poetry is prayer. Poets themselves are conscious in varying degrees of their aims; some write, like Milton, with a carefully formulated purpose; others 'pipe but as the linnet sings', like the author of *Songs of Innocence*; some, like Coleridge, bring their poems to birth 'as recollection or the drug decides'. And poetry acts upon the reader in various ways: a poem may please our ears, it may feed our imaginations, it may stir our emotions; it may, for a moment or for much more than a moment, alter profoundly our consciousness of the world around us and our attitude towards it.

Speaking for myself, I must say that the more I think about literature, the harder it becomes to define it and its subordinate provinces, and the less profitable any attempt at a precise or logical definition

B [17]

seems to be. The boundaries that divide prose from poetry, for instance, and poetry from verse, become shadowy under inspection and disappear. And so it is with greatness; many things have been suggested by critics as its essential mark—originality of mind, imaginative power, nobility of nature, power of influencing others; one cannot say, about greatness any more than about poetry itself, that there is one right way of using the word and all other ways of using it are wrong. Therefore I shall not attempt to impose a definition, but shall rather try simply to sort out my impressions in the light, so to speak, of my own linguistic habits, and to trace them to their source in the writer or his work.

You may have noticed that though I have spoken of great poets, I have so far refrained from speaking of great poetry. And this has been instinctive; the word 'great' suggests itself to me less easily in connexion with a work than with a writer; it does not come naturally to me to speak of a great line, a great stanza, or a great sonnet. If I do this, nine times out of ten it is no more than a careless and emphatic way of saying that I think the line or passage in question especially moving or impressive; it is not 'true' greatness that I am thinking of.

If I do, so to speak, catch myself out attributing 'true' greatness to a poem, I find on reflection that it is usually to a work on a large scale, not to a couplet, an epigram, or a sonnet; and on further reflection it almost always turns out that in calling it great I was really thinking more about the author than about the work itself; that what impelled me to call it great (as would be the case if I called it a masterpiece, or a work of genius) was something much more closely connected with its author, much more directly and fully expressive of something in him, than is (say) its beauty or technical perfection. Of course, it is to its author that a work of art owes all its attributes; it is what it is because he, being what he was, made it so. But some of the qualities we attribute to a work of art are really qualities not of the work but of its creator; when we say that a work is 'original' (for instance) or 'daring' we are really speaking as much about the creator as about the work itself; and when we call a poem great I do not think that the word has any meaning except by reference to an author, actual or supposed.

Great Poetry

A very simple test convinces me of this. Suppose a line of poetry strikes me as beautiful, and I am then told that the sequence of words that it consists of came together purely by chance, or as the result of a typographical confusion; I should not, in that event, alter my judgment and think that it was any the less beautiful a line for that. But if I had judged it to be great, then the news that the sequence of words that it consists of came into existence quite fortuitously would, I think, cause me to change my opinion; to call a chance collocation of words an example of poetic greatness would simply, to my way of thinking, be nonsense.[1]

Common speech lends support to this view of the matter: we do not naturally call a sunset, or a fine mountain panorama, 'great', however beautiful or 'glorious' we think it, however deeply we are affected by its beauty. And that, surely, is because there is no author to whom we can refer it—the view from my window is a landscape without a painter, the sunset is a poem without a poet. It is not because it is not a work of art, for things other than works of art—an action, or even, in certain contexts, a gesture—can affect us with this sense of greatness just as authentically as does a picture or a poem. It is because the landscape and the sunset do not—like the action or the gesture—reflect a personality.

If you think of Nature as expressing the personality of the Creator, then you may indeed call a landscape great:

> *The spacious firmament on high*
> *With all the blue ethereal sky*
> *The spangled Heavens, a shining frame,*
> *Their great Original proclaim.*

Addison might have called a sunset, or the night sky, 'great', but that is because to him Creation proclaimed its great Original.

[1] There are difficulties about the view that greatness is really attributable to the author rather than to the work. Can a work of composite authorship—say, the *Iliad*—be great? Must we wait till we know the authorship of a poem before we can judge whether it is great or not? What about forgeries? What about the poem that is the product of automatic writing? These difficulties disappear if we suppose that when we think of a work of art as great there is always a suppressed protasis in our thought: 'This is a great work *if and in so far as it is the sincere product of a single mind.*' I insert 'sincere' in order to exclude pastiche and forgery.

Great Poetry

Of course it is upon his poetry that a poet's title to greatness rests: there are no mute inglorious Miltons—or, rather, the mute Miltons remain inglorious—and since it is through his poems that we come to know the poet's greatness it is only natural to apply the epithet to his work as well as to himself.

And of course the word 'great' is very commonly applied to poems, as it is to poets, simply as an epithet of vague laudation. *The Ancient Mariner* and *The Rape of the Lock*, Gray's *Elegy* and *The Waste Land*, *Lycidas* and *The Lotus Eaters*—all these would no doubt qualify for inclusion in a collection of Great Poems; each of them is an example of poetic excellence of one kind or another. This is simply the popular notion of greatness—established excellence—used with reference to the poem instead of to the poet. But on reflection, we distinguish between 'great' poems just as we do between 'great' poets; we recognize a difference between the merely excellent on the one hand and the 'truly' great on the other. *The Rape of the Lock* is a perfect poem; but is it great as *Tintern Abbey* is great? *The Vanity of Human Wishes* is a splendid poem; is it 'truly' great, like *Samson Agonistes*?

Reflecting, then, on my instinctive use of the word 'great' in connexion with poetry, I find that I associate it naturally with the author rather than with his work, and that when I apply it to the work it is something about the author that I have in mind. Critics have not always approached the matter in this way. From the time of Aristotle until the end of the eighteenth century, they looked upon greatness as a quality inhering in the poem itself, and necessarily connected with its subject: a poem could not be great, they concluded, unless its subject was sublime.[1]

'A Heroick Poem, truly such,' says Dryden, 'is undoubtedly the greatest work which the Soul of Man is capable to perform. . . . The action of it is always one, entire and great. . . . Even the least portions

[1] 'Their [the Greeks'] theory and practice alike, the admirable treatise of Aristotle, and the unrivalled works of their poets, exclaim with a thousand tongues—"All depends upon the subject; choose a fitting action, penetrate yourself with the feeling of its situations; this done, everything else will follow"' (M. Arnold, Preface to the 'New Edition' of his *Poems*, 1853).

... must be of the Epick kind; all things must be Grave, Majestical, and Sublime.' 'The file of Heroick Poets', he goes on to tell us, 'is very short. There have been but one great *Ilias*, and one *Aeneis*, in so many ages. . . . *Spencer* has a better plea for *Fairy-Queen*, had his action been finish'd, or had been one. And *Milton*, if the Devil had not been his Heroe, instead of *Adam*.'

Dr. Johnson had no doubts about the greatness of *Paradise Lost*: 'considered with respect to design,' he says, '[it] may claim the first place, and with respect to performance the second, among the productions of the human mind.' True, in discussing it he speaks of Milton's 'appetite for greatness' and tells us that 'The poet, whatever be done, is always great'; but even when he says this he has his eye not on the man but on the poem and its subject: 'The subject of an epic poem is naturally an event of great importance. That of Milton is . . . the fate of worlds. . . . Great events can be hastened or retarded only by persons of elevated dignity. Before the greatness displayed in Milton's poem all other greatness shrinks away.' What is the greatness displayed? Is it Milton's greatness? No: it is the greatness of the subject: 'The weakest of his agents are the highest and noblest of human beings, the original parents of mankind.' If Milton is great it is simply because he can rise to the heights of this exalted theme: 'The characteristick quality of his poem is sublimity. He sometimes descends to the elegant, but his element is the great.'[1]

Of course, even critics in the classical tradition did not judge the greatness of a poem by reference simply to its subject: they required the poet to display powers of invention and execution worthy of his theme;[2] and there was one lonely critic who burst the bonds of that

---

[1] 'He can occasionally invest himself with grace, but his natural port is gigantick loftiness. Algarotti [he adds in a note] terms it *gigantesca sublimità Miltoniana*.'

[2] Johnson himself, at the close of his Milton essay, hints at the need for something more than judgement and skill in execution: 'the highest praise of genius', he declares, 'is original invention'; *Paradise Lost* is 'not the greatest of heroick poems, only because it is not the first'. The remark is thrown in almost as a postscript: if Johnson had stayed to develop it, he would surely have perceived that, unless by original invention he meant mere novelty, he was admitting that greatness was an attribute primarily of the poet himself and only secondarily of his work. Even so, he would no doubt have maintained that it could only be exhibited by treating a subject

tradition and sought the source of greatness in the author himself. Longinus—that figure of mystery, who is never mentioned by any classical writer, whose treatise lay hid until the Renaissance had run its course (it was not published until the middle of the sixteenth century) and to whom Boileau and Pope paid lip-service but nothing more—Longinus placed first among the elements of sublimity in literature—before intensity of emotion, skill in composition, taste in expression, and all the classical armoury—grandeur of conception; and grandeur of conception was for him a quality existing not in what is conceived but in the mind or nature that conceives it: ὕψος— he declared—μεγαλοφροσύνης ἀπήχημα: Sublimity is the echo of greatness of mind.

To see the greatness of a poem as the reflection of something in the poet's mind, to conceive of the poet as conferring greatness on his theme and not, so to speak, as living (or writing) up to its inherent greatness—before that idea could take possession of English criticism there had to be a revolution in the critic's way of looking at his subject.

The author of this revolution—so far as any individual deserves the credit for it—was Coleridge. There are many strands in the texture of Coleridge's criticism; indeed to talk of 'texture' is to pay it a compliment it hardly deserves—it is too often a tangle of unfinished thoughts, crossing and contradicting each other, impossible to reconcile, and hard enough sometimes even to elucidate. But in one clear conviction Coleridge never wavered: the poem could not be judged apart from its author. 'What is poetry? is so nearly the same question, with what is a poet? that the answer to one is involved in the solution of the other.' And the greatness of the poet's work depends, according to Coleridge, upon the profundity of his mind: 'No man was ever yet a great poet, without being at the same time a profound philosopher.'[1] Of course Coleridge is not using the word 'philosopher' in any technical sense; he does not mean that the

of adequate sublimity: 'great events ... hastened or retarded by persons of elevated dignity'—a poet could prove his greatness only by writing on such themes as these.

[1] Characteristically, he blurs the clarity of this by adding an unhelpful metaphor: 'For poetry is the blossom and fragrance of all human knowledge, human thoughts, human passions, emotions, language.' This is really very little better than William Michael Rossetti.

greatness of a poet depends on the validity of his metaphysics. What he requires as an element of 'original poetic genius' is, in his own words, 'depth and energy of thought'.

It is not surprising that Coleridge's approach to the greatness of *Paradise Lost* was the opposite of Dr. Johnson's: 'In the *Paradise Lost*', he says, 'the sublimest parts are revelations of Milton's own mind, producing itself and evolving its own greatness. . . . In all modern poetry', he continues, there is 'a fleeting away of external things, the mind or subject greater than the object; the reflective character predominant.'

Even as Coleridge was writing, a change was making itself felt in English literature, and that change reflected his own philosophical temper,[1] his incorrigible tendency to take large views, his terrible appetite for ideas, and his morbidly sensitive and introspective temperament. A wider range of subjects, a greater variety of methods of treatment, became accessible to writers. Poetry, and literature generally, came to be thought of less as a craft and more as a means of self-expression. That was why the nineteenth century saw an unprecedented flowering of the personal lyric and the novel—the literary forms in which the writer can most fully and freely express his deepest feelings and convey his attitude towards human nature and life at large.

Walter Pater seized on this distinctive character of his own age when in his essay on Charles Lamb he suggested that the temper of the nineteenth century was to be distinguished from that of the

---

[1] Coleridge's own ideal of an epic poem was so high as to be unattainable. Writing to his friend Joseph Cottle, he tells him how he would prepare for the composition of an epic:

'I should not think of devoting less than twenty years to an epic poem. Ten years to collect materials and warm my mind with universal science. I would be a tolerable mathematician. I would thoroughly understand Mechanics; Hydrostatics; Optics, and Astronomy; Botany, Metallurgy; Fossilism; Chemistry; Geology; Anatomy; Medicine; then the mind of Man; then the minds of men, in all Travels, Voyages and Histories. So I would spend ten years; the next five in the composition of the poem, and the last five in the revision of it.'

We have come far, in a dozen years, from Dr. Johnson. No need, now, for the great poet to choose 'persons of elevated dignity', to treat them in a style of 'gigantic loftiness'. Not that, indeed, but how much more, is now required of him!

eighteenth by a 'deeper subjectivity', an 'intenser and closer living with itself'.

In prose, one can trace this increasing subjectivity from *Peregrine Pickle*, through *Persuasion* and *The Egoist* and *The Golden Bowl*, to *Ulysses* and the novels of Virginia Woolf. One can trace it in verse from *The Task* through *The Prelude* and *In Memoriam* and *Modern Love* to *The Waste Land*.

No one today would dream of suggesting that the greatness of a piece of writing depended on the inherent sublimity of its subject. If we look for greatness, for instance, in Thomas Hardy, we are as ready to find it in his lyrics as in *The Dynasts*, among great events and 'persons of elevated dignity'.[1]

This change of outlook can be traced very clearly in the criticism of Matthew Arnold. In the Preface to the first collection of his *Poems*, published when he was barely thirty, Arnold stated the classic, the Aristotelian, the Johnsonian doctrine with hardly a qualification:

'I fearlessly assert [he declared] that Hermann and Dorothea, Childe Harold, Jocelyn, The Excursion, leave the reader cold in comparison with the effect produced upon him by the latter books of the Iliad, by the Oresteia, or by the episode of Dido. And why is this?

---

[1] It is a strange thing that Pater, who preached so persuasively the gospel of art for its own sake, should have believed that the greatness of a work of art depends upon its subject, and that he should have declared this belief at the end of his 'Essay on Style'—the essay in which he expounded the doctrine that music 'is the ideal of art precisely because in music it is impossible to distinguish the form from the substance or matter, the subject from the expression'. Having defined 'the condition . . . of all good art', he proceeds:

'Good art, but not necessarily great art; the distinction between great art and good art depending immediately, as regards literature at all events, not on its form, but on the matter. . . . It is on the quality of the matter it informs or controls, its compass, its variety, its alliance to great ends, or the depth of the note of revolt, or the largeness of hope in it, that the greatness of literary art depends, as *The Divine Comedy, Paradise Lost, Les Misérables, The English Bible*, are great art.'

I cannot quote the passage in full, or enter into the difficulties it entails. The description of great art seems at once too broad (can *'The English Bible'*, any more than *The Golden Treasury*, be a great work of art?) and too narrow (for it must be limited to literature, as Pater seems to be aware, uneasily). It reads almost as if it were inserted at the end of the essay as an after-thought.

[24]

Simply because in the three latter cases the action is greater, the personages nobler, the situations more intense: and this is the true basis of the interest in a poetical work, and this alone.'[1]

Now it is both a merit and a defect in Arnold that he always writes as if he were arguing, he has always vividly before him a man he wants to convince, and something he wants to convince him of. This keeps his style alive, but it tempts him to overstatement. And in this Preface, his desire to refute the then current doctrine that 'the Poet ... must leave the exhausted past, and draw his subjects from matters of present import'—a view that is still with us (the poet must 'be contemporary', must 'express his age', must 'reflect the contemporary consciousness'), a view of which I would say, like Arnold, 'This view I believe to be completely false'—Arnold's desire, I say, to refute this view led him to overstate the virtues of the ancients, the classical writers of Greece and Rome, to embrace too readily the classical view of poetic greatness, and to assert, as he does without qualification, what he calls 'the all-importance of the choice of a subject'.

Ten years or so later, Arnold had come to take a different view. It was in the 'Lectures on Translating Homer', delivered in 1861–2, that he offered his famous definition of the Grand Style: 'The Grand Style', he said, 'arises whenever a noble nature poetically gifted treats with simplicity or severity a serious subject.' And Arnold went on to say that Homer worked *entirely* in the grand style, and to offer Homer, Virgil, Dante, and Milton as 'eminent specimens' of that style.

Now to say this is surely to get yourself into a difficulty.[2] Homer is

[1] Arnold goes on to oppose himself expressly to the subjective tendency described above: 'The modern critic not only permits a false practice; he absolutely prescribes false aims. "A true allegory of the state of one's own mind in a representative history", the Poet is told, "is perhaps the highest thing that one can attempt in the way of poetry." And accordingly he attempts it. An allegory of the state of one's own mind, the highest problem of an art which imitates actions! No, assuredly, it is not, it never can be so: no great poetical work has ever been produced with such an aim.'

[2] As later critics pointed out: see Saintsbury, 'Shakespeare and the Grand Style', in *Essays and Studies by Members of the English Association*, i, 1910; John Bailey, 'The Grand Style: An attempt at a Definition', ibid., ii, 1911; and Saintsbury, 'Dante and the Grand Style', ibid., iii, 1912.

capable of grandeur, but to say that he is always grand is to use the word in an unnatural sense. Homer and Virgil resemble each other, no doubt, in many respects, but one respect in which they do not resemble each other is style. Dante and Milton have much in common; a style is one thing they do not have in common. And Arnold failed, I think, to rescue himself from that difficulty by his device of dividing his 'Grand Style' into two grand styles—the 'grand style simple' and 'the grand style severe'—which in fact have no common quality, least of all grandeur.

The truth is that Arnold's conclusions, again, were coloured—one might say vitiated—by the context in which he was speaking. He was really thinking about poetic greatness, but he was preoccupied with style because his immediate business was to demonstrate to his audience the right kind of style for a translation of Homer, who happened to be (in his view) a great poet. The poets he chose as his examples, the passages he offered as touchstones, are by no means all of them specimens of the grand style; but they are all of them examples of poetic greatness. And this fact, which shows itself between the lines in the 'Lectures on Translating Homer',[1] emerges clearly in the three later essays in which he speaks his last word on the subject.[2]

In his essay on Wordsworth, Arnold picks up his phrase of nearly twenty years before and displays it in a different light. 'Long ago,' he says, 'in speaking of Homer, I said that the noble and profound application of ideas to life is the most essential part of poetic greatness.' It is true; he did say so, but only in passing, almost parenthetically, in the course of his attempt to define the grand style. What was then offered as the criterion of the grand style is now

[1] There is a significant sentence in the Lectures on Homer; Arnold says that 'the insurmountable obstacle to believing the Iliad a consolidated work of several poets is this—that the work of great masters is unique; and the Iliad has a great master's genuine stamp, and that stamp is the *grand style*'.

[2] These three essays appeared in successive years: the preface to his selection from Wordsworth in 1879, the General Introduction to Ward's *English Poets* in 1880, and the preface to his selection from Byron in 1881. All these were reprinted in the second series of *Essays in Criticism* which came out, just after his death, in 1888—the very year in which Pater's 'Essay on Style' appeared in *The Fortnightly*.

explicitly made the criterion of the great poet, for he goes on, 'A great poet receives his distinctive character of superiority from his application, under the conditions immutably fixed by the laws of poetic beauty and poetic truth, from his application, I say, to his subject, whatever it may be, of the ideas "On man, on nature, and on human life", which he has acquired for himself.' What he is now seeking to define is the great poet, not the grand style; and subject, once 'all-important', has receded to the background—'whatever the subject may be'.

A page or two later comes the dictum, 'It is important, therefore, to hold fast to this: that poetry is at bottom a criticism of life; that the greatness of a poet'—it is the *great* poet that he is concerned with —'lies in his powerful and beautiful application of ideas to life, to the question: How to live'.

This famous pronouncement dominated English criticism till the end of the nineteenth century; since then it has come under heavy fire. The element in it that has drawn that fire has been, of course, the ethical element—the suggestion that it is the poet's business to teach us how to live. Arnold was himself at pains to disclaim any such doctrine; he protested that he did not mean to say that the poet was concerned to inculcate a system of morals, or that poetry was essentially didactic—nor, indeed, was that what Arnold did say. He said that the poet's greatness consisted not in teaching us how to live, but in the 'powerful and beautiful application of ideas' to that question—a very different thing from the providing of an answer to it. 'A large sense', he declared, 'is of course to be given to the term *moral*. Whatever bears upon the question, "how to live", comes under it.'

One must not probe too deeply into Arnold's analysis; he did not, perhaps, ask himself very clearly what he meant by the 'subject' of a poem or by the 'application' of ideas to a question, and the possibility of writing an entirely 'pure' or 'abstract' poetry, never, no doubt, entered his mind. But the importance of 'subject' in any limited sense seems to diminish at each stage of his thought on the matter. He said that a serious subject was a pre-requisite of the grand style; but, later, that a poet's greatness springs from his application of certain ideas to his subject 'whatever it may be'; and, finally, that greatness

[27]

lies simply in the powerful and beautiful application of ideas to life. I think he would have been inclined—and increasingly inclined—to say that the greatness of a poem depends upon what the poet brings to his subject, and not upon that subject's inherent sublimity.

The doctrine of the 'subjectiveness' of the subject is pushed almost to its extreme limit by Henry James.

'The one measure of the worth of a given subject, [says James] the question about it that, rightly answered, disposes of all others—[is] "Is it valid, in a word, is it genuine, is it sincere, the result of some direct impression or perception of life?" . . . There is [he continues] no more nutritive or suggestive truth in this connexion than that of the effect dependence of the 'moral' sense of a work of art on the amount of felt life concerned in producing it. The question comes back thus, obviously, to the kind and degree of the artist's prime sensibility, which is the soil out of which his subject springs. The quality and capacity of that soil, its ability to 'grow' with due freshness and straightness any vision of life, represents, strongly or weakly, the projected morality. That element is but another name for the more or less close connexion of the subject with some mark made on the intelligence, with some sincere experience.'[1]

Plainly James did not think of the subject as something lying outside the work itself, as a piece (as it were) of reality that the work represents or describes.[2] For him there was the thing seen or felt or

[1] From the preface to *The Portrait of a Lady* in the New York edition of James's works. James continues:
'The house of fiction has in short not one window, but a million—a number of pierceable windows not to be reckoned, rather; every one of which has been pierced, or is still pierceable in its vast front, by the need of the individual vision and by the pressure of the individual will . . . at each of them stands a figure with a pair of eyes. . . . The spreading field, the human scene, is the "choice of subject"; the pierced aperture, either broad or balconied, or slit-like and low-browed, is the "literary form"; but they are, singly or together, as nothing without the posted presence of the watcher—without, in other words, the consciousness of the artist. Tell me what the artist is, and I will tell you of what he has *been* conscious. Thereby I shall express to you at once his boundless freedom and his "moral" reference.'

[2] To say that a work of art has a subject is, surely, to say, at the least, that its creator recognizes, if not refers to, a reality outside the work itself. The precise meaning of the word varies according to the *genre* the work belongs

heard about; there was the artist's sensibility; there was the work itself—the 'subject' was what the writer made of his experience; in a work of the creative imagination it was indistinguishable from the substance of the work: the subject of *The Wings of the Dove* was the imagined experience of Milly Theale, not the real experience of Minnie Temple.

If, then, greatness is, or ultimately depends upon, something in the artist's nature or sensibility, what is that 'something'? What is it in the artist, writer, or poet, that distinguishes him as great? Let me make clear my method of approaching this question. I am not allotting marks or awarding prizes; I am not even making any judgment about literary merit; I am not saying who 'deserves' to be

to; a portrait is 'of' its subject; a poem is probably best described as being 'about' its subject, where it can be said to have one. A discussion of the meaning of 'subject' in literature might well take the form of a discussion of the various possible meanings of the word 'about'. Sometimes what we call the subject is no more than a theme, sometimes (in some lyrics, for instance) it is barely even that, only an occasion. How many subjects has a novel?

The difficulty of identifying anything as its subject often makes it hard for the poet to find a title for a lyric; and the abstract painter, who rejects all reference to external reality, is in the same dilemma. So, writing of his picture 'Boon' (T 253 in the Tate Gallery), James Brooks declares:

'The painting is completely abstract—having been developed from an improvised start and held into a non-figurative channel. As to the title, the name originates as identification only, but generally the painting and the title share a kind of meaning later. I used to number my paintings, then later letter them, calling them A, B, or C, down to Z, purely according to their sequence in that year of production. Neither of these systems worked well. Neither I nor anyone else could remember individual paintings by that system.

'Now I use the same sequence, but complete the initial with a made-up word, without too much attention to its evocative value, depending on its long association with the picture to develop a meaning. The titles are an attempt to avoid a name whose associations will be read into the picture.'

Evidently the artist is afraid that if he gives his picture a significant, evocative title, the picture will acquire a subject (for the spectator) from that title (a strange reversal of the ordinary process whereby the title is derived from the subject); it therefore has to be given a null title, yet one different enough from other titles to be remembered in association with the picture; then, somehow, 'a meaning' for the picture 'develops' from that association.

called great; I am simply looking for the common quality or combination of qualities that distinguishes those to whom I—and, I
imagine, most critics, would instinctively and unreflectingly apply
the title—say, Shakespeare, Milton, Wordsworth, Dante, Virgil,
Sophocles.

'One knows fairly well what one means by great art', wrote Ezra
Pound; 'One means something more or less proportionate to one's
experience. . . . It is for some such reason that all criticism should be
professedly personal criticism. In the end the critic can only say "I
like it", or "I am moved", or something of that sort. When he has
shown us himself we are able to understand him.' 'Thus, in painting',
Pound continues, 'I mean something or other vaguely associated in
my mind with work labelled Dürer, and Rembrandt, and Velasquez.
. . . And in poetry I mean something or other associated with the
names of a dozen or more writers'.[1] Very well; but the critic must, as
Pound half admits, say more than 'I am moved'; he must show us
what it is that moves him, and explain the 'something' that his 'great'
painters and writers have in common. For myself, the best explanation I can give is this: *if a poet persuades me by his poetry that he has
looked deep into things; that, so looking, he sees them as somehow parts
of a universal whole; and that he has responded to this vision with an
appropriate emotion; and if the poetry by which he persuades me of this
moves me as poetry—then, and only then, I would call him great.*[2]

The great poet need not, of course, be a philosophical or a religious
poet; he need not be, in the ordinary relations of life, what we call a
good man. But he must persuade me by his poetry, whatever its subject, of his insight into 'the architecture of life', and of the adequacy
of his natural response to what he sees.

If that is the great poet, great poetry is simply the poetry,

[1] 'The Serious Artist', in *Literary Essays*, 1954, pp. 55–56. Pound is less
happy when he attempts a 'closer analysis', identifying great art with
'maximum efficiency of expression', and holding it to be 'of necessity a
part of good art'.

[2] It is necessary to add the proviso, 'If his poetry moves me as poetry',
because there is no reason in the nature of things, as far as I can see, why a
man who possesses the other qualifications of a great poet should possess
also the peculiar power of communicating his vision in poetic form. The
potentially great poet might be a bad poet, and our description must be
framed so as to exclude him.

whatever its subject, by which such a poet makes me aware of his greatness.

The elements that, on this view, go to make poetic greatness may be variously combined, and may be displayed in varying degrees at different points in a poet's work; and it makes sense to say that of two great poets one is greater than another. But plainly this is a field in which precise measurement and precise definition are impossible, and if two critics disagree about whether a particular poet is great or not, there is no way of proving that one of them is right and the other wrong. If I am asked to define depth of insight, I can do so no more than Matthew Arnold could define what he meant by nobility of nature; if anyone asks what is an appropriate emotional response, I can only say, as Arnold said of the grand style, that you must feel it in order to know what it is.

There is a school of thought that would banish from criticism words that refer to attributes whose presence cannot be checked, and their extent measured, by criteria which all would accept as valid. The great, the beautiful, the noble, the cheap, the vulgar, the sentimental—such terms find no place in scientific criticism and discussion of them can amount to no more than a comparison of personal impressions. Greatness, as I have tried to describe it, is certainly such a conception, and some of the terms one is compelled to use in trying to elucidate it may be so uncertain in their connotation as to be, strictly, meaningless; using them, one cannot prove or convince. But there is surely a middle course between the nebulous raptures of Swinburne on the one hand and 'the submission of silent wonder' on the other. Reflecting upon poetry with these ideas in mind, one may at least clear up dark places in one's own thought and learn to choose and arrange one's words so that they are not self-contradictory; one may reveal fresh aspects and features of poetry, to one's self and others.

If one reaches a definition or description of the category of the great by reflecting on examples that clearly fall within it, one can best test it by considering cases falling on its border-line.

Let me begin with one whom Ben Jonson called 'the first poet in the world for some things'. John Donne was certainly that, and he was something more than that. His poetry was a vivid expression of his strong and strange personality; by means of it he really altered not only the way that poets wrote but the way that people felt towards each other all over England for nearly a hundred years.

But, searching Donne's poems from end to end, I nowhere find that sense of the universal which seems to me a necessary note of greatness; the ardour of his passion, and his unremitting introspection, do not allow him ever, either in his love-poems or in his religious poetry, to forget himself and the object of his devotion. He is, perhaps, too personal a poet to be great. Compare him with his contemporary Shakespeare: Shakespeare founded no school, and impressed himself so little on his work that we have not the faintest idea what he was like. But to compare Donne with Shakespeare is to see the difference between a great poet and one who is merely superb.

A great poet must be able to lose or to forget his own personality; he must be capable of being calm; ardour, one might almost say, is the enemy of greatness. That, perhaps, is why so few love-poets have been 'truly' great in their lyrical expression of their own passion (does Shakespeare prove his greatness *in this sense* by his Sonnets, 'great' though, plainly, they often are in the ordinary sense of the word?), and why some of the most intense and moving of devotional poets fall short of 'true' greatness. There is no more exciting, no more passionate, love-poet in any language than Catullus; but if you set him beside Virgil you will instantly see that Virgil has an insight, a depth of vision, and a range of imagination for which you will search Catullus in vain. Devotional poetry touched great heights in Crashaw and in Christina Rossetti; set the one beside Milton and the other beside Wordsworth and you become aware of a whole world of feeling that is closed to their intensity.

Poetic genius is one thing, poetic greatness is another. Blake was, I suppose, a genius; he was also—I would not dispute Housman's judgment—the most poetical of English poets. And he abounds in gnomic utterances of an apocalyptic kind:

> *To see a World in a grain of sand*
> *And a Heaven in a wild flower.*

Great Poetry

But Blake was a visionary: I am not persuaded by his poetry that he was anything but a passive vehicle for his visions, when he says that what he wrote was dictated to him by an angel he speaks the truth, and he is denying his own claim to greatness.

Take an example from the novel. Trollope was at least as copious in invention as Tolstoy, he had as sharp an eye, he was as adept in the shaping and telling of a story—in the mechanics of his art. But no one would dream of calling him a great novelist in the sense in which Tolstoy was great. And that is not because Tolstoy worked on a large canvas, described earth-shaking events, and spread himself in philosophical reflections upon them. It is because Tolstoy saw deeply into life, while Trollope only copied it.

There is no end to the series of examples one could take, and to test this or any other such description by applying it to individual writers is certainly an amusing and may be an instructive game. But to make the game worth playing, to throw fresh light on the qualities of the writers chosen or on the implications of the description itself, one would have to examine each example more closely than is possible in a single hour. I would rather use the time available in considering how the writer by using words, and other creative artists by using other media, are able to achieve greatness of this kind.[1]

In ordinary speech, we apply the word 'great' to the painter, the musician, the sculptor, the architect, as readily as we apply it to the writer of poetry or prose; and we apply it to all of them without distinction, taking it for granted, apparently, that they may all be great in

---

[1] I pass by the interesting question how far 'real'—like 'popular'—greatness can be achieved in other than artistic fields. The general, the judge, the statesman, the mathematician—can these be truly great in the same sense as the poet and the painter? And what of the performers and interpreters—the actor, the dancer, the musical conductor or executant? In each case the test, it seems, must be: does his *métier* allow him to express the richness of his nature and the depth of his vision of life? Was Newton, in this sense, great? was Einstein? was Capablanca? Each was, in his own field of intellect, a genius. To have revolutionized thought in any field implies, no doubt, imagination and intellectual courage, and (if the field is an extensive one—I doubt if the chess-board is wide enough) some vision of the universe; but does it require any richness of nature or the capacity for noble emotions?

C

[33]

the same way. If we are giving the word 'great' its popular meaning, no difficulty arises: of course an artist, whatever his medium, can in his own field be excellent or eminent. But is the same true of 'real' greatness, as we have described it? Can those other artists persuade us by their art of their insight into the unity of things and of the adequacy of their response to what they see? Can a man, simply by arranging sounds or shapes or lines or coloured surfaces, convey to us his reading of life and his attitude towards it, as the writer can convey them by arranging words?

The writer, because his medium is more fully articulate than theirs, might seem to be better equipped than other artists for recording his insight into reality and conveying to others his feelings about it. Of his rivals, the painter has a more promising medium than the musician, for if he is a 'figurative' and not an 'abstract' painter he can work upon our emotions by representing, or suggesting, or reminding us of scenes and objects, people and life.[1] And this the painter does, though it is often hard to say how much a picture's effect upon us is due to the representation, to the 'subject' and its associations, how much to its purely visual element, and how much to the relations between the two, to the fact that this scene, this object, is presented to us in just this way.

'And yet it is beautiful,' wrote Virginia Woolf of a sordid interior by Sickert, 'satisfactory; complete in some way. Perhaps it is the flash of the stuffed birds in the glass case, or the relation of the chest of drawers to the woman's body; anyhow, there is a quality in that picture which makes me feel that though the publican is done for, and his disillusion complete, still in the other world of which he is mysteriously a part without knowing it, beauty and order prevail; all is right there'—or, as she sums it up in a single sentence, 'the chest of drawers and the arm convince us that all is well with the world as a whole'.

What Virginia Woolf is describing is not greatness but the painter's mysterious power—a power displayed by many painters who are far

[1] How far is 'representational' art imitative, and how far is it simply suggestive, of 'reality'? Does the figurative painter make something that is 'like' what his picture represents, or does he create a set of conditions which cheat us, so to speak, into thinking that it is so? These are interesting and difficult questions, but irrelevant to the present inquiry.

from being 'great'—of delighting us, moving us, exhilarating us, appealing to our sense of beauty and order, enhancing our sense of the value of life.[1]

The painter can do this by placing the arm in a right relation to the chest of drawers; he can do it by painting a landscape or a still life—the flash of the stuffed birds in the glass case—he can do it, even, by a purely abstract and non-representational picture. For apparently the human frame is so constructed that certain combinations of colours and forms, and certain features (for instance, symmetry, repetition, and particular space relations) in what is presented to our eyes, affect not only our senses but our emotions, and they can do this without any reference to external 'reality'—no need of the bird, the glass case, the arm, the chest of drawers. A simpler age explained this as an effect of mystical or mathematical virtues inherent in the visual pattern; fuller knowledge suggests that we should look for the cause rather, or also, in our own visceral and nervous organization. Whatever the explanation (if, indeed, anything that is really an explanation is possible), it is the fact that we can be genuinely and deeply moved and excited by a purely abstract

[1] Matthew Arnold in his essay on *Maurice de Guérin* (written before 1865) describes this power; he is speaking of poetry, but what he says describes equally well, if not better, the power of the painter—he might be writing about a still-life by Cézanne:

'The grand power of poetry is its interpretative power; by which I mean, not a power of drawing out in black and white an explanation of the mystery of the universe, but the power of so dealing with things as to awaken in us a wonderfully full, new, and intimate sense of them; and of our relations with them. When this sense is awakened in us, as to objects without us, we feel ourselves to be in contact with the essential nature of these objects, to be no longer bewildered and oppressed by them, but to have their secret and to be in harmony with them; and this feeling calms and satisfies us as no other can. Poetry, indeed, interprets in another way besides this; but one of its two ways of interpreting, of exercising its highest power, is by awakening this sense in us. I will not now inquire whether this sense is illusive, whether it can be proved not to be illusive, whether it does absolutely make us possess the real nature of things; all I say is, that poetry can awaken it in us, and that to awaken it is one of the highest powers of poetry.'

I must repeat, that Arnold here is describing, as it seems to me, the peculiar power of the creative artist—not the special attribute of the great artist. To the great artist belongs, perhaps, that 'other way' of 'interpreting', which Arnold refers to, but does not describe.

work of art[1] or by a chance collocation of things seen in nature itself
—a cluster of pebbles on the beach or clouds in the sky, or a con-
stellation of splashes on the wall.

It is true also that the unmeaning lines and forms of the non-
figurative artist may possess a splendour or refinement or meanness
or vulgarity that betrays something of his inner self; he may reveal
himself through them as he might through his aimless scribbles on
the blotting-paper.[2]

But if he is to achieve greatness as I have described it, the artist
must do more than excite us, or lay bare his personality; he must
convey to us the depth of his insight into life, and the adequacy of
his response to what he sees. And that is what a really great painter
manages to do; that is what Rembrandt does, for instance, by his
'Prodigal Son' in the Hermitage and by his self-portrait at Ken
Wood; that is what Titian does by his 'Pietà' in the Accademia and
Tintoretto by his 'Crucifixion' in the Scuola di S. Rocco. It can be
done by a painter of landscapes—Turner does it—perhaps, more
mysteriously, by a painter of still-lives. But can it be done by a purely
'abstract' painter, who renounces all reference to reality, including
the distortion of it? I dare not be dogmatic, but it appears to me that
the answer must be 'No'. A great picture must have some recognizable, intelligible, reference to a reality outside itself.

The case of music seems to be very different. The composer,

---

[1] We *can* be; but of course many—probably most—of the people, and
not only the young people, who say that they are moved or excited by an
'abstract' work of art (and the same is true of their professed reaction to
analogous works of literature) are not so moved at all; they are simply
pretending, and their pretence often deceives themselves as well as others.
They are moved by a desire not to be, or be thought, *arrière-garde*; by
mere considerations of fashion; and (often) by a genuine taste for novelty
and adventure and a distaste for the conventional and the accepted as
such. And, *mutatis mutandis*, exactly the same is true of many—probably
most—of the people, and not only the old people, who say that they are
deeply moved by the Old Masters, or by Shakespeare.

[2] Character and personality reveal themselves also in our bodies, and not
only in the organs that express, or undergo change in accompaniment to,
our emotions: 'His jaw was too square and set and his figure too straight
and stiff: these things suggested a want of easy consonance with the
deeper rhythms of life.' We do not have to look far among our own
acquaintance to find the mean ear, the brute nose, and the criminal back.

though his is the most abstract of all arts,[1] for his medium does not enable him to convey thoughts or represent objects, can, despite the apparent intractability of his medium, achieve that greatness which is open to the figurative artist or to the poet, who has language at his disposal. Beethoven not only was a more accomplished composer than (say) Clementi, he saw more deeply into life and responded more nobly to what he saw. And we are convinced of this without the interposition between the composer and ourselves of a single word, or thought, or idea, or reference to a reality outside the work itself, simply by listening to the sequences of sounds that he designed. Beethoven's greatness as a composer consists in his power of persuading us by means of his music of the nobility of his vision of life.[2]

The painter's apparent advantage, then, would seem to be illusory; indeed, the advantage is with the musician, who in his entirely abstract medium can achieve something that is beyond the power of the 'abstract' painter, something that a painter can only achieve if he uses a figurative, representational art.

I see no reason why we should be surprised by this state of affairs. It is due simply to the way we are made—the luck, so to speak, of the senses: they do not all stand (why, after all, should they?) on the same footing in this respect. Critics, perplexed and dissatisfied, have tried to persuade themselves and others that it is not so. Thoré, for instance, more than a hundred years ago, suggested that perfumes could be as expressive as lines or colours, and he envisaged an *art des parfums* which would enable him to stage scent-dramas, addressed to the audience (if 'audience' is the right word) solely through their sense of smell.[3] But unfortunately sight and hearing are in this

[1] Architecture approaches music in this respect, and approaches it the more closely the nearer it is itself to pure decoration. But architecture may be more or less intimately connected with practical human purposes, and it is easier to see how an architect could communicate his insight into life and his attitude towards it by planning a city than to see how he could communicate it by designing an obelisk.

[2] Clementi's reading of life may, of course, have been as profound as Beethoven's; but his failure to persuade us of this by means of his music prevents him from being accounted as great a composer.

[3] 'Avec les parfums on peut exprimer toute la création aussi bien qu'avec les lignes ou la couleur. . . . Seulement la peinture et la sculpture représentent directement les objets . . . tandis que les parfums, comme la

[37]

respect far ahead of the other senses, and to hold that they are all on the same footing as artistic media, and that 'abstract' visual art must therefore be capable of exercising as great a sway over our emotions as music, is simply another manifestation of the hopeful egalitarianism of the present day.

What, then, in this matter is the position of the writer? A glance at the other arts has suggested that their practitioners can convey to us a reading of life and the nature of their response to it, without having recourse to the intellect—or at any rate to its discursive faculty. The painter, it is true, may have to call in the aid of representation, and much of his power to move us springs from a recognizable reference to a reality external to his work; but the musician dispenses with even that much of reference to 'reality'; and neither of them uses a word[1] or conveys a thought.

The writer's medium is language, and words are our most efficient means of conveying thoughts and ideas, and are used more often in order to convey them[2] than for any other purpose. The writer can tell us articulately and explicitly what he sees in things and what he thinks and feels about them. Of course, especially if he is a poet, he often uses words for other purposes than conveying thoughts, and there has been a strong tendency, ever since the days of the Symbolists, to exalt the non-intellectual functions of words in poetry—their evocative and suggestive power and their power to move us simply by their sound and through the appeal of rhythm and metre to the ear. Critics and poets have been led to exalt or exploit these powers of language partly in revolt from Arnold's supposed doctrine that poetry should be a criticism of life, partly as a result of

musique, reveillent l'intuition des choses. . . . Vous jouerez des drames, des comédies et même des vaudevilles en parfums' (Thoré, *L'Art des Parfums*, 1836).

[1] The composer of songs or operas or 'programme music' avails himself, of course, of words and action which make an explicit reference to an external reality. But the great musician *can* achieve his effect without any such reference.

[2] Or to conceal them—but then by conveying other thoughts or ideas. Of course, words are rarely used in order to convey thought and nothing else; but they are so used sometimes, e.g. in legal documents and scientific treatises.

discoveries in psychology, and partly under the influence of French symbolist doctrines which set up the abstract art of music as a model for poets. It has even been suggested that a poet ought to purge his work of all intellectual content as of an impurity, and that by so doing he will exalt it to the condition of the pure art of music.

Poetry, we are reminded by these doctrinaires, is written not with ideas, but with words. The epigram is attractive, but the antithesis it states is misleading. It is often taken to mean that poetry is written not with ideas but with sounds. In fact poetry is written with symbols that stand for sounds of a particular kind, those sounds which by convention convey ideas and compose articulate speech. So the epigram should be restated: poetry is made up not only of sounds but also of ideas—'ideas' including thoughts and the whole world of images that the use of words can evoke. Of course, that restatement tells us only what has in fact been the practice of most poets in the past; there is no reason why a poet, if he wishes, should not exclude from his writing, to a greater or lesser degree, the intellectual element; he need not make statements; he may give us a succession of images without intelligible connexion; or, like Gertrude Stein, a succession of words strung together with little grammatical connexion and with meaning hammered out of them by repetition; or, like the Russian futurists who invented a 'trans-sense' language of their own to which there is no dictionary, a rigmarole from which every trace of significance has vanished. A poet may, if he wishes, do any of these things; there is no need to provide him with any justification—least of all the false one that because the poet moves us by something else besides what he actually tells us, and because other artists move us without telling us anything at all, the poet ought to try to move us without telling us anything at all, and that the less he tells us the purer, and the more like music, his poetry will be.

The idea that if you remove from poetry the intellectual element what is left is music, or something in the nature of music, is demonstrably false. The test is simple: read a poem—I will not weight the scales unfairly by choosing an intellectual and cacophonous poet like Donne, but (say) a series of Pope's heroic couplets or a stanza of Swinburne at his most melodious—read such a poem to someone ignorant of the English language. He may well derive pleasure from what he hears, but that pleasure will have nothing (except that it reaches him through the ear) in common with the pleasure he would derive from hearing a concert of orchestral music or a tune played on a single instrument. He hears spoken words, not notes or combinations of notes.

Of course an artist in language can so use it as to give pleasure to the ear. But a great deal of the pleasure that, listening to poetry, we think purely auditory, is in truth dependent on our understanding what the sounds stand for—it is the pleasure of recognition, of appreciating the *rightness* of the sound.[1] And although it is true that there is a song, a heard pattern, in poetry, it is not a purely auditory pattern; it cannot be fully appreciated unless the hearer understands what is being said. A certain rhythm pleases us as contributing to the expression of a certain sentiment; the pleasure to the ear of pause, suspension, emphasis, rise and fall, depends upon their being placed rightly with reference to the sense.[2]

It is not always because they are vainly aspiring to attain to the 'condition of music' that poets reduce the intelligible element in their work. Sometimes they are reproducing, more or less exactly, the flow of images through a dreaming mind; sometimes attempting to convey, more directly than can be done by statement, their feelings, physical or emotional; sometimes invoking the symbolic potency of certain images or ideas. Traditional poets have done all these things, without throwing the discursive intellect overboard, or abandoning a

[1]   *Lo, where Maeotis sleeps, and hardly flows*
          The freezing Tanais through a waste of snows—
What we may call the exquisite beauty of the sound of these lines would not be appreciated by someone who did not know what they meant. And to one who did not know English the sound of them would give, at best, a very, very faint indication of what that meaning is. Some words may sound whiter or colder than others, but that is as far as we can go.

[2] 'My true love hath my heart and I have his': substitute the word 'lover' for 'true love' and the poetical effect of the line is ruined. This is not because of the change in sense, which is nugatory; nor because of the change in sound, for to one who did not understand the sense, the one line sounds as musical as the other; it is because a slight metrical irregularity— a spondee for an iamb in the second foot, an extra accent on 'love'—gives us two long lingering syllables at a point where, the meaning being what it is, they are emotionally effective.

more or less dominant intelligible scheme or subject. If we analyse their work we often find that it owes its effectiveness far more to the unintelligible than to the intelligible element in it. But in the last half-century, poets have gone much farther along these lines than ever before, and strange and effective experiments have been made in the abandonment of meaning.

Such poets renounce—as does the abstract painter—the chief weapon in their armoury, their main link with the reader's mind. But that, after all, is their affair, and they have every right to insist on being judged simply by the results that they produce; if they can move us or intrigue us by their phantasmagoria of images, by a verbal pattern, or by the mysterious communication of a mood, it is beside the point to complain that their method is illegitimate or that the result presents 'difficulties'—or impossibilities—to the discursive intellect, to which it never was addressed.

Yet one may wonder whether, by denying himself three-quarters of the potentiality of his medium, by abolishing subject and intelligible reference to a recognizable reality outside his work, the poet has not disabled himself from achieving greatness of the kind we have been discussing.

> *Now*
> *Say nay,*
> *Sir no say,*
> *Death to the yes*
> *The yes to death, the yesman and the answer,*
> *Should he who split his children with a cure*
> *Have brotherless his sister on the handsaw.*

That is a careful pattern. But it is difficult to see how poetry composed entirely of patterns such as that can communicate a reading of life, a vision of reality; the insight, if insight there is, remains private to the author.

Here are the opening lines of another poem by the same writer:

> *Because the pleasure-bird whistles after the hot wires,*
> *Shall the blind horse sing sweeter?*
> *Convenient bird and beast lie lodged to suffer*
> *The supper and knives of a mood.*

[41]

That is a sample of poetry that affects the reader by a succession of images which have little or no intelligible connexion with each other or recognizable reference to a world common to the poet and his reader. By means of a body of work in this manner a poet might give us a panorama of his imaginative world, much as he might by telling us a long succession of his dreams; and strong threads of personality might run through the tapestry and colour it; so that, like the dream-teller, he might in this way convey to us something about himself. He might excite us by his imagery and intrigue us by suggestions of symbolism. But if Dylan Thomas had written always in this manner, I do not think he could have communicated his insight into life and his response to it in such a way as to persuade us of his greatness, and I wait to be convinced by example that such a poet can be great.

It does not follow, of course, from what I have said about the need for communication that it is by directly or intelligibly communicating their vision or describing their response to it that the great poets persuade us of their greatness. Wordsworth is continually reminding us of the source from which his greatness springs—his sense of 'something far more deeply interfused', his power of seeing 'into the life of things', his sensitivity to the influence of natural objects. But it is not when he tells us of this most directly, when he presents himself as the bearer of a message, that he most persuades us that he is a great poet.

> *One impulse from a vernal wood*
> *May teach us more of man*
> *Of moral evil and of good*
> *Than all the sages can.*

There is Wordsworth's message, the secret of his greatness, un-folded plain for all to see. But if you listen carefully to that trans-mission of the message, you will perceive that the line goes dead after the first half-dozen words—a stanza begun by Wordsworth has been completed by Longfellow. A line of poetry is followed by three lines of doggerel.

'One impulse from a vernal wood'—those words alone (they make no statement, they do not even form a sentence) are enough to convey the insight and the response that, expressed in verse, impel us to call Wordsworth a great poet. The very word 'impulse' in its context in that line really contains all that we are explicitly told in the three lines that follow about the teachability of moral good and evil.

That line of poetry was evoked simply by 'the influence of natural objects'; take now two stanzas that express feeling for another human being; the nature of the insight, the quality of the emotion, are the same, but here the poetry is sustained throughout the whole short poem:

> *A slumber did my spirit seal;*
>   *I had no human fears:*
> *She seemed a thing that could not feel*
>   *The touch of earthly years.*
>
> *No motion has she now, no force;*
>   *She neither hears nor sees,*
> *Rolled round in earth's diurnal course*
>   *With rocks, and stones, and trees.*

I cannot imagine clearer or more perfect evidence of poetic greatness —insight, apprehension of an underlying unity in things, and a fitting emotional response poetically rendered.

I say 'evidence', for when we call poetry 'great' we are saying that it is a revelation of the greatness of the poet who wrote it. And here a troublesome question presents itself. How many such lines or poems must a man write to prove himself a great poet? Twenty poems, or half a dozen? A hundred lines, or fifty? Or would a single authentic poem, a single line of really great poetry, suffice to qualify him for the title?

If this is asked about greatness in the popular sense it is, I think, a frivolous question. We all feel, when we try to estimate the greatness that consists merely in eminence, that scale or size, magnitude of achievement, has something to do with it; and we all realize, surely, that it would be a waste of time to attempt to lay down any standard.

But if the questioner has in mind true greatness, if he means 'How many such lines, or poems, of Wordsworth must we read before we can be certain of his greatness?' then his question—though it is no more capable of a precise answer—is not a frivolous one, and deserves serious consideration.

A poet's potentialities, his sensitiveness, the quality of his emotion in the face of ultimate realities, may reveal themselves, more or less completely, in a single poem, a single stanza, a single line or phrase—'One impulse from a vernal wood.' 'To be right in great and memorable moments is perhaps the thing we should most desire for ourselves', said George Eliot: such moments may reveal the man.

But a moment is only a moment, and inspiration is fitful, and the great line may, I suppose, come once in a lifetime; it may even be a freak, and not represent the writer's true, his constant, self: 'Great lines by bad poets' would be an interesting study, and raise a difficult aesthetic problem.

Perhaps it is fortunate that I have no time to deal with puzzles such as these; but they will explain my reluctance to speak of a great poem or a great line—why I am tempted to say 'There is no great poetry; there are only great poets'. And I would answer the question 'How many such lines or poems must one read before one can safely call their author great?' by asking 'How many brave acts must a man perform before we can safely call him a brave man?'—'Enough', the answer must be, 'to enable us to recognize his courageous nature.' The full realization of a poet's greatness comes upon us gradually; we acquire our conviction of it cumulatively, by reading individual works or passages in his work; it is his power, fitful though it may be, of producing such work that constitutes his greatness: once appreciated, we can recognize it in a line or in a phrase.

The elements of poetic greatness, I have said, may be variously mixed. If Wordsworth is great by virtue of his power of vision, the greatness of Yeats proceeded rather from the richness of his nature, of his response to what he saw.

Yeats was certainly a great poet, and not only in the popular sense. More than that, he looked and conducted himself like a great poet; he had no doubt that he was one. He was, in the ordinary relations of life, a remarkable mixture of shrewdness and gullibility, of the vain and the magnanimous, the practical and the romantic. His personality was powerful, and he impressed it upon his work; he created

a language and a world of his own. He left a large body of passionate
and moving poetry recording his adventures in many fields of action,
thought, and emotion. The richness of his imagination and the
magnificence of his purely poetical gifts tended to overlay and obscure—as I think they did with Shakespeare—the special gift of
communicating his sense of the fundamental unity behind appear-
ances. It is rarely that he seems to go straight to the centre of things.
But I think he does this in, for instance, *The Cold Heaven*:

> *Suddenly I saw the cold and rook-delighting heaven*
> *That seemed as though ice burned and was but the more ice,*
> *And thereupon imagination and heart were driven*
> *So wild that every casual thought of that and this*
> *Vanished, and left but memories, that should be out of season*
> *With the hot blood of youth, of love crossed long ago;*
> *And I took all the blame out of all sense and reason,*
> *Until I cried and trembled and rocked to and fro,*
> *Riddled with light. Ah! when the ghost begins to quicken,*
> *Confusion of the death-bed over, is it sent*
> *Out naked on the roads, as the books say, and stricken*
> *By the injustice of the skies for punishment?*

There is a poem that concerns 'the influence of natural objects'
and conveys the poet's insight into nature as surely as anything
Wordsworth ever wrote, and with more eloquence and imaginative
power than Wordsworth could command.

The richness of nature that is a chief element in Yeats's greatness
as a poet shows itself clearly in these stanzas from *A Dialogue of Self
and Soul*:

My Soul. Such fullness in that quarter overflows
> *And falls into the basin of the mind*
> *That man is stricken deaf and dumb and blind,*
> *For intellect no longer knows*
> *Is from the Ought, or Knower from the Known—*
> *That is to say, ascends to Heaven;*
> *Only the dead can be forgiven;*
> *But when I think of that my tongue's a stone.*

My Self. *A living man is blind and drinks his drop.*
What matter if the ditches are impure?
What matter if I live it all once more?
Endure that toil of growing up;
The ignominy of boyhood; the distress
Of boyhood changing into man;
The unfinished man and his pain
Brought face to face with his own clumsiness;

The finished man among his enemies?—
I am content to follow to its source,
Every event in action or in thought;
Measure the lot; forgive myself the lot!
When such as I cast out remorse
So great a sweetness flows into the breast
We must laugh and we must sing,
We are blest by everything
Everything we look upon is blest.

'The echo of a mighty mind,' 'the reflection of a noble nature': those phrases might, surely, have been coined to describe such poetry as that.

A noble nature: that, according to Matthew Arnold, is the first essential of a great poet. I have preferred to speak, less vividly and perhaps more vaguely, of the poet's appropriate response to his vision of the universe. But by substituting a colourless phrase for Arnold's 'noble' I have hidden, not eliminated, a metaphysical or moral judgment that cannot in the end be avoided.

Whether you intend it or not, whether you know it or not, whether you like it or not, by calling a poet or a poem great you are implying a judgment about the universe of which he and it are a part, and about the attitude that befits a human being who is aware of his situation in it.

If you say of a poet merely that he is excellent, or call his poem beautiful, or say that it has moved you, you imply no such judgment —indeed, if you say that you find a poem moving, perhaps you are, strictly, not making a judgment about the poem at all.

Great Poetry

The difference between the description I have offered and that proposed by Arnold reflects rather a diversity of point of view than a divergence in critical judgment. My list of great poets would probably not differ much from his, and my reasons for calling them great are not so very different; it is partly that nowadays we are more fully aware of the unconscious foundations of our aesthetic judgments, partly that, being less confidently high-minded, we tend to express ourselves in less overtly ethical terms.

Arnold's references to the poet's noble nature and to the seriousness of his subject suggest requirements which we certainly do not acknowledge. True, the great poet must be capable of noble moments, he must see his subject in a universal context; but he need not be a saint or (*pace* Coleridge) a philosopher—and my description is intended to emphasize this. Perhaps the emphasis is superfluous—for, after all, Arnold did not really believe that Homer must have been a good man or that it is impossible to write great poetry about a primrose. What he did believe, and what we, consciously or unconsciously, are implying when we call a poet or a poem great, is that the universe makes serious demands upon us and it is unworthy of a human being to dismiss it as a trivial affair. The great artist—poet, painter, composer of music—persuades us of this, and of his awareness of it, by playing each in his own way upon our minds and upon our senses.

Medieval Latin Poetry[1]

In the course of his peregrinations through Italy, the humanist Flavio Biondo visited the legendary abode of the Cumaean Sibyl. He describes the scene of desolation that lay before him: all was in ruins; 'et ubi Apollinis arx fuit, sacellum est Christianum, et ipsum vetustate consumptum'. *Et ipsum vetustate consumptum*—that mouldering shrine might be taken for a symbol of the Latin poetry of the Middle Ages: the edifice of Christian verse which had supplanted the poetry of pagan Rome was now itself in decay, and the humanist, looking back from the threshold of one golden age of art over the ten long centuries that separated it from its predecessor, could see nothing but one ruin piled upon another.

A different image may suggest itself to the critic who today attempts to trace the course of poetry across that long millennium: he may rather be reminded of a flight by aeroplane over the deserts and mountain ranges of the Middle East. As the trackless, treeless wastes unroll themselves, from sunrise to sunset, from sunset to sunrise, the traveller finds himself wondering at the harsh prodigality of a Creator who could allow so great a proportion of a finite universe to remain inaccessible to any kind of cultivation: one is journeying, it seems, through a world devoid alike of life and of art. Then the aeroplane dips, and with a closer vision one can detect, here and there, a patch of green, a stretch of something like a road, the fragments of a wall or a hut, something *made*, something moving, something actually alive—a herd of goats, perhaps, or bony mountain sheep, and then—miracle of miracles!—little figures which we know that we should recognize, if we could but get close enough to them, as human beings.

[1] Review of *A History of Secular Latin Poetry* by F. J. E. Raby, 1958.

[48]

Medieval Latin Poetry

Something like that may well be the uninstructed reader's first impression of the vast tracts of medieval Latin verse that present themselves in (for example) Polycarp Leyser's *Historia Poetarum Medii Aevi*, or in the *Poetae Latini Aevi Carolini*, or in Migne's *Patrologia*. This, it is true, is a literary panorama; the 'desert' is itself the work of man's hands; but it offers to the eye of the uninstructed traveller the same repulsive features as does its geographic counterpart: vast tracts whose monotony is broken only by recurrences of the grotesque; a thin soil spread over a crude, strange surface; no gracious evidence of any truly civilized or civilizing hand.

Dr. Raby has performed a valuable service to literature by making this vast and forbidding territory of medieval verse accessible to the ordinary inquirer; under his guidance, it becomes an interesting and intelligible, if not an attractive, landscape; and when he introduces us to its inhabitants, when we begin to read in detail, we realize that it is peopled by human beings like—or almost like—ourselves.

More than thirty years ago, in his *History of Christian Latin Poetry*, Dr. Raby dealt with the religious element in this literature, tracing its development 'not merely from the point of view of form and technical structure, but also in relation to the religious and intellectual conditions under which it was produced', and showing 'in what different countries, under what various cultural traditions, and in relation to what changing religious outlooks, the vast body of Catholic poetry was built up by the labour of more than a thousand years'. He followed this up with a study of secular verse, identical in scope and purpose, a second edition of which is now before us. After twenty-five years, Dr. Raby has found hardly anything to alter in his book and very little to add to it, beyond bringing his bibliography up to date and giving an account of two collections of songs recently made available from manuscripts in the University libraries of Oxford and of Cambridge.

Dr. Raby's two great works (for they deserve that title) are learned and comprehensive; they are at once a history and a critical study of the Latin poetry of the period; they contain a full bibliography and (in effect) a copious anthology; and they are written in an easy style, free from any trace of pedantry. Together, they constitute one of

D   [49]

the major achievements of English twentieth-century scholarship.

The interest taken nowadays in medieval Latin, as has been observed by Professor Beare, is 'an interest coloured by a certain degree of emotionalism'—an emotionalism which, in his view, has had unfortunate results in the field of philology and metrics. Its results are no less apparent in the field of literary criticism. Just as proconsuls often evince a paternal tenderness for the races among which they have spent a lifetime of administration, so scholars—particularly if they are men, like Dr. Raby, of human sympathies—incline to an undue partiality for the period and the literature that have occupied their working life: 'their' authors become their *protégés*. So medievalists (misled, perhaps, by the light of the false dawns which preceded it) seem inclined to deplore, if not actually to deny, the fact of the Renaissance, and to exalt the children of their darkness at the expense of the adult figures of the Enlightenment. Dr. Raby does not fall into this error; he is as sound a critic as he is an historian; he knows good poetry when he sees it, and bad poetry too, and he makes no exaggerated claims for the poets of his period.

Analysing 'the creation of the medieval outlook', Dr. Raby traces from Gorgias to Apuleius, and beyond, that rhetorical tradition under the influence of which poetry 'lost the breath of life' and became 'an affair of the schools' and the poet, writing (whether in Greek or in Latin) in an entirely 'literary' language, sought to astonish rather than to move, to impress others rather than to express himself. 'The so-called Silver Age,' says Dr. Raby, 'is the age of rhetorical poetry, and this poetry lasted as long as the schools of rhetoric and their successors existed in the West, that is, until the end of the Middle Ages.' Rhetoric and true poetry are not incompatible—was not Virgil equally a rhetorician and a poet?—but when rhetoric prevailed it opened the way to a world of 'topics', of pedantry and affectation, of antithesis and 'wit', which at its worst displayed itself in acrostichal and telestichal verses, 'figured' poems made in the shape of the objects they described, verses every word of which begins with the same letter, or which can be read indifferently backwards and forwards, and the other toys in which the Middle Ages never ceased to take delight. So the rhetorical tradition corrupted what it

[50]

preserved of the classics, and for a thousand years men worshipped Virgil—and used his works simply as a quarry for their centos.

But there was another influence in the field—the influence of rhythmical prose, and in particular of the liturgical 'sequence'. From this grew up a new religious and romantic poetry which gradually supplanted the traditional Latin verse, and in the end itself gave place—or should one say 'gave rise'?—to the vernacular poetries of Europe. It is in this 'popular' kind of verse, in which accent displaces quantity, and assonance and rhyme play an increasing part, that most of the great medieval Latin hymns and almost all the best-known and most admired secular lyrics of the period were written.

Before a stream of truly medieval verse could begin to flow through those two channels, the Classical spirit had to die; and the process was a long one. It is not until the beginning of the seventh century, says Dr. Raby, that 'the direct contact or continuity with classical antiquity appears to be on the point of vanishing' and 'a world which bears all the marks that we are accustomed to associate with the Middle Ages is making its appearance'. Then followed a period of 'intellectual barrenness and decline'. A thin thread of culture was preserved by the Church; the library of Isidore of Seville, for instance, was stocked with classical and sacred texts, concerning which he pleasingly observed:

> *sunt hic plura sacra, sunt hic mundalia plura,*
>   *ex his si qua placent carmina, tolle, lege.*
> *prata vides plena spinis, et copia florum :*
>   *si non vis spinas sumere, sume rosas.*

But in his own century the roses were few and far between. Surveying the Spanish poets of the time—Eugenius of Toledo and the 'poet-kings' Sisebut, Chintila, Wamba and the rest—Dr. Raby has to admit a 'decline in skill and even in taste', 'a defective sense of quantity and a lack of discrimination in the choice of words'; Gaul in the same period presents (he says) 'a sorry tale', and 'the story of Italy is not dissimilar'.

By now, however, rhythmic verse was growing side by side with the classical quantitative metres. 'Something new and grand had

[51]

come into being,' says Dr. Raby, 'something that could not have grown on Latin soil'; and he quotes from the best-known example of such poetry, the 'Altus prosator', attributed to St. Columbia:

> *girans certis ambagibus*
> *redit priscis reditibus,*
> *oriens post biennium*
> *Vesperugo in vesperum;*
> *sumpta in proplesmatibus*
> *tropicis intellectibus.*

'Verse of this grandeur is rare,' says Dr. Raby. That may be; but readers of the 'Altus prosator'—it is nearly 300 lines long—are not likely to complain of short measure.

At the end of the eighth century came the first of the false dawns—the Carolingian 'renaissance'. Real learning flourished at the court of Charles, the classical metres were cultivated, and Theodulph wrote flowing elegiacs on a wide range of topics. But Dr. Raby has not rescued from all the production, quantitative and rhythmical, of the Court poets—apart from one or two touching pieces by Alcuin and a few lines by Paulinus of Aquileia—anything that one could honestly describe as poetry, anything that, except for the sake of curiosity, one would wish to read a second time.

Rhythmical poetry flourished especially, it seems, outside the circle of the Court. These poems were for the most part made to be sung; for metre, they often depend only on equality in the number of syllables, and rhyme is fitful; but the beat of the accent and the faint assonance could at times produce a strangely moving effect. Here is the opening of a dirge on the death of the great King:

> *A solis ortu usque ad occidua*
> *littora maris planctus pulsat pectora.*
> *hei mihi misero!*

There is something haunting about that. But after half a dozen stanzas the poet has sunk to such stuff as

> *imperatorem iam serenum Karolum*
> *telluris tegit titulatus tumulus—*

and long before the poem ends the reader will have laid the doggerel wearily aside.

The ninth century—the aftermath of the Carolingian revival—can show 'few good poets': Irish influence on the Continent, particularly the baneful influence of John Scotus Erigena, was strong; the Irish were scholars, and their pupils liked to parade their learning, particularly in Greek, not always with fortunate effects. Here is Sedulius Scottus, one of the most prolific of them, describing the normal activities of a learned and easy-going monk:

> *aut lego vel scribo, doceo scrutorve sophiam:*
> *obsecro celsithronum nocte dieque meum.*
> *vescor, poto libens, rithmizans invoco Musas,*
> *dormisco stertens: oro deum vigilans.*

His invocations of the deity were answered, one hopes, more favourably than his invocations of the Muse, for this is a poem which, Dr. Raby tells us, shows Sedulius's talent 'at its best and happiest'.

Contemporary with Sedulius were Hincmar and Hucbald, the latter of whom wrote a long poem on baldness from which Dr. Raby selects 'perhaps the best passage':

> *carmina, clarisonae, calvis cantate, Camenae.*
> *comperies calvos columen conferre cerebro;*
> *comperies calvos capitis curare catarrhos;*
> *comperies calvos caecas curare catervas,*
> *cronica cum cancro ceditque cacexia calvo;*
> *cardia cor carpens cassatur, colica cessat.*

Medieval readers looked upon such verses not as monstrosities but as delightful poetry: 'hoc scriptum carmen complet dulcedine mentem' is the marginal comment of a contemporary copyist.

A purer strain of poetry is to be found in the occasional poems of Walafrid Strabo; his little hexameter piece on his garden stands half-way between the *Georgics* and later didactic poems on the same topic, like those of Rapin and Cowley *De Plantis*; its modest charm lies in its attention to the practical details of its subject, the purity of its language and the regularity of its metre.

The tenth century is pre-eminently the century of epic and

historical poetry—evidence of the growth throughout Europe of national feeling. There is the *poeta Saxo*, a 'poor but well-meaning versifier', who chronicled the exploits of Charles the Great; and the monk Abbo who wrote an account of the siege of Paris by the Normans; and the long Waltharius epic, a Latin expansion, influenced by Statius, of a Hunnish legend; and finally there are 'the laboured verses of the *Ecbasis Captivi*, an anonymous beast-epic, told . . . as a moral tale' in leonine hexameters, largely compounded of scraps from classical and Christian poets. Dr. Raby has digested all these works (and many more), and expounds them to us without losing his good humour or his critical sense of proportion.

Then there are (mercifully) shorter poems such as those of Eugenius Vulgaris, who sought to please his Imperial and Papal patrons with poems designed to display his accomplishment as a dialectician:

> *Si sol est, et lux est; at sol est; igitur lux.*
> *si non sol, non lux est; at lux est; igitur sol—*

and so on.

Sometimes a rhythmical lyric seems to spring from a genuinely poetic impulse, as in two famous anonymous anthology pieces, both from Italy:

> *O Roma nobilis, orbis et domina*
> *cunctarum urbium excellentissima,*
> *roseo martyrum sanguine rubea,*
> *albis et virginum liliis candida :*
> *salutem dicimus tibi per omnia—*

and the love-lyric from the Cambridge song-book:

> *O admirabile Veneris idolum.*

But in neither lyric—and the failing is a frequent one in the verse of the time—can the poet sustain his opening impulse, and after half a dozen lines the lover is thus addressing the object of his affection:

> *'Salvato puerum' non per ipotesim,*
> *sed firmo pectore deprecor Lachesim,*
> *sororem Atropos, ne curet heresim.*

Medieval Latin Poetry

Neptunum comitem habeas et Tetim,
cum vectus fueris per fluvium Tesim.

Others would read *Saluto puerum*; but nothing will turn 'non per ipotesim' into poetry, or redeem the gaucherie, both of feeling and of expression, in the lines that follow.

Occasionally, as in the strangely moving *Carmen Mutinense*, meant to be chanted on the battlements of a city during the night watches—

O tu qui servas armis ista moenia
noli dormire, moneo, sed vigila!—

a relentlessly recurring monorhyme is used to good effect.

In the eleventh century—'a century of preparation and promise', says Dr. Raby—the Carolingian learning was continued in cathedral schools of the Continent; the Sequence, which infused into verse—first religious, then secular—something of the freedom of rhythmical prose, reached perfection; and Hildebert of Lavardin extended the possibilities of rhyme.

So Dr. Raby reaches the twelfth century, the century of Abelard and Adam of St. Victor, and, in secular verse, of the *Carmina Burana* and the Goliards. After that come Aquinas and Jacopone da Todi; then there is anti-climax: in the words of Dr. Brittain, 'the pale after-glow of the glorious sunset of the thirteenth century': the breath of life had departed from Latin verse and was transfused into the new vernacular poetries.

The impression left by Dr. Raby's survey—one can hardly repro-duce it in a brief summary, still less convey the masterly manner in which he deals with the vast mass of material and the innumerable historical and literary problems that present themselves *en route*—is that the secular poetry of the Middle Ages was a gallimaufry of learning and childishness, degenerating at times into pedantry and barbarism, with recognizable human feeling breaking through ever and anon, but rarely finding an adequate means of expression in the stunted vocabulary and graceless metres of the time. The panorama that seemed from far off to be a barren desert turns out to be a wilder-ness, covered with scrub and cactus, starred here and there with a

[55]

wild flower. One is astonished to find how much verse was written during the Dark and Middle Ages, and how little of it is worth preserving for its own sake.

The scraps quoted above have not been selected with a view to depreciating the achievement of medieval versifiers—far less favourable specimens might have been chosen: we have spared the reader the horrors of Virgilius Maro and the *Hisperica Famina*, the puerilities of John the Deacon and the tedious inanities of Dudo of St. Quentin and a hundred others. Our aim has been to give a fair impression of the background so fully set out by Dr. Raby, against which one should view the poetical successes of the age.

For of course the age had its successes, and they were in two fields: liturgical verse and the personal lyric—indeed, to judge from most anthologies, one would suppose that little else was written by the poets of the Middle Age, and it is important that that distortion should be corrected.

Religious poetry lies outside the scope of Dr. Raby's present book, but (as he constantly reminds us) the two elements in the edifice of medieval verse cannot really be kept apart. It was in the austere yet touching measures of Ambrose, the bold rhythmical experiments of Notker and his contemporaries, and the exalted anthems of Abelard and Adam of St. Victor and the anonymous hymnologists of the twelfth and thirteenth centuries, that the medieval spirit found its most successful medium of poetic expression. Incorporated into the liturgy, their hymns survived into the Renaissance, when the secular poetry of the Middle Age had become a dead letter. Under Leo X, Ferreri classicized the hymns in the Breviary by substituting versions in quantitative measures, but the effort was stillborn; the old versions were retained, and the revisers under Urban VIII contented themselves with correcting only the most obvious solecisms. Since then, *Dies irae, Lauda Sion salvatorem, Dulcis Jesu memoria, O quanta qualia,* with scores of other sacred songs, have become part of the poetic, and not merely the religious, heritage of western Europe.

Yet a doubt obtrudes itself. Are they really finer than the best of our own hymns—'When I survey the wondrous Cross', 'Jesu, where'er thy people meet', 'O God, our help in ages past'? Our metres are simpler and fewer, but they allow a greater variety and beauty of effect. 'Upon the fall of their Empire,' said Dryden, 'the Romans doted into rhyme, as appears sufficiently by the Hymns of the Latin Church,' and Dr. Raby admits that the leonine hexameter was a disastrous invention. But it was not only in quantitative metres that the effect of rhyme was unfortunate, it too often turned accentual verses into jingles. For the poet who would rhyme in Latin is in a dilemma that arises from the shortage of monosyllables and the exigencies of an inflected language: single-syllable rhymes tend to be mere assonances (e.g., duell*o*, mirand*o*, ov*es*, peccator*es*, in a sequence of Wipo), while two-syllable and three-syllable rhymes are usually, at least to English ears, not rhymes at all. The greatest of the Latin hymns are marred by such effects as the following, from *Dies irae*:

> *Confutatis maledictis*
> *flammis acribus addictis,*
> *voca me cum benedictis.*

One wonders whether the poignancy of their opening phrases— 'Dies irae,' 'Stabat mater dolorosa'—the solemnity of their themes, the associations with which they are encrusted, and our memory of the surroundings in which they are sung and the beauty of the chants to which they are set, have not won for these moving hymns a pre-eminence which they could not claim simply as poetry.

As for the secular lyric, its range is wider, but it rarely achieves the same intensity of emotional effect. Leaving aside cheerful monkish doggerel—

> *multi sunt presbyteri qui ignorant quare*
> *super domum domini gallus solet stare*—

the dog-Latin of uproarious schoolboys in the 'Dulce Domum' vein—

> *Ferulae frangantur*
> *totum est de festo,*
> *virgae non promantur,*
> *via sumus praesto*—

and the jovial obscenities of much of the Goliardic verse, we are left with a handful of love-lyrics, some from the tenth century, preserved in the famous Cambridge collection, more belonging to the twelfth, from the still more famous collection of Benediktbeuren, others to which can be attached the name of an individual author, like the touching 'O quid iubes, pusiole' of Gotteschalk. Almost all are in accentual metres, adorned with rhyme, and many breathe a gentle charm recalling a tapestry of the Garden of Love. Their kinship with the lyrics of *le fin amour* is obvious, especially when vernacular and Latin poems are printed side by side, as in Dr. Brittain's anthology *The Mediaeval Latin and Romance Lyric*. But they are simple things, touching us with something of the pathos of a child's speech, and we must not make exaggerated claims when comparing them with the adult poetry of classical times or of the post-Renaissance centuries.

Here are the *Verna Suspiria* that an anonymous song-writer puts into the mouth of a love-lorn maiden:

> *Levis exsurgit zephyrus*
> *et sol procedit tepidus;*
> *jam terra sinus aperit,*
> *dulcore suo diffluit . . .*
>
> *cum mihi sola sedeo*
> *et haec revolvens palleo,*
> *si forte caput sublevo,*
> *nec audio nec video.*

The simplicity of the words, and above all of the word-order, is strangely effective. Is it deliberate? Or is the poet unselfconscious, the feeling only half-realized? Or is it that the language is too simple for emotions that it seeks to, but cannot quite, express? For the effectiveness is that of broken English, or the speech of a peasant or a child. Indeed, it has been claimed that Medieval Latin—with its limited vocabulary, its simple syntax and word-order, its inadequate means for expressing the oblique—is the peasant speech of Rome, surviving the literary language of the classics. Dr. Raby might with profit have enlarged on the question how far the substance of medieval poetry was determined by the limitations of the language in which it was written.

However that may be, one need only contrast

[58]

Medieval Latin Poetry

si forte caput sublevo,
nec audio nec video

with a stanza of Catullus:

tenuis sub artus
flamma demanat, sonitu suopte
tintinant aures, gemina teguntur
lumina nocte—

to see that the classical (like the modern) poet is capable of a deeper analysis of a lover's emotions and has at his disposal a fuller and subtler medium for expressing them.

In their refusal to admit the limitations, linguistic and emotional, of medieval verse, in their insistence on endowing these poets with a false 'modernity', some of their worthiest champions (notably Miss Waddell and, more recently, Dr. Bolgar) have done them a disservice. 'The culture of the twelfth century,' says Dr. Bolgar, in his learned survey of *The Classical Heritage*, 'represents for the first time the lineaments of modern man. . . . *L'homme moyen sensuel* makes his bow in the songs of the so-called wandering scholars. . . . All shades of sexual emotion . . . all the varied attitudes that spring from appetite and ambition, are present in this literary heritage.' To prove his point he quotes from one of the most famous and admired of medieval poems, 'Meum est propositum in taberna mori':

Presul discretissime, veniam te precor :
morte bona morior, dulci nece necor,
meum pectus sauciat puellarum decor,
et quas tactu nequeo, saltem mente moechor.

'This is a far more successful analysis,' declares Dr. Bolgar, 'than we shall get in the several hundred pages of the *Éducation Sentimentale*.'

What comment is possible on such a judgment? It is but an extreme example of the tendency noted above: a deluded parent is inviting us to admire the precocity of his backward child, and we can only greet his praises with an embarrassed silence. It is to Dr. Raby's credit that he nowhere yields to the prevailing tendency, but allows the Middle Ages to remain medieval and spares us such embarrassments as this.

The Seventeenth-Century Background[1]

What, we may ask, is the background of an age? It depends, no doubt, on the point of view of the observer. For many historical or literary inquirers a mass of material details composes the background against which they see the figures that they study—an assemblage of crinolines, stage-coaches, warming-pans, wigs, sedan-chairs, coffee-houses, pillories, maypoles, ruffs, portcullises and other such appendages of living. We are conscious, with a degree of vividness proportionate to our imagination and our antiquarian knowledge, that it was on a stage set with such properties as these that battles were fought, books written and laws enacted.

The seventeenth-century background presented to us by Mr. Basil Willey is of a very different sort from that. For him the physical conditions of life are relegated to the foreground, where they become mere detail and lose their importance in the picture, like flowers or insects in the painting of a landscape; they are to be overlooked while we fix our eyes on a larger, mistier, mountainous scene—the background of ideas against which the men of the seventeenth century lived their lives. Mr. Willey deals with a background of thought; or rather with an intellectual atmosphere, to which those who breathed it owed (in a large measure, we need not doubt, unconsciously) their life and their strength, and only in the light of which we can understand them fully. He studies the varying 'climates of opinion' in an age when opinion was radically changing, a century in which the transition in England from a 'medieval' to a 'modern' view of the universe was effected. 'The Rejection of Scholasticism', 'Bacon and the Rehabilitation of Nature', 'The Philosophical Quest for Truth',

[1] A review of *The Seventeenth-Century Background*, by Basil Willey, 1934.

[60]

The Seventeenth-Century Background

'Rational Theology', 'The Heroic Poem in a Scientific Age'—these chapter headings give some idea of the point of view from which Mr. Willey looks upon England between the day of Bacon and the day of Locke. They are profoundly interesting topics, and he treats them brilliantly. His concentration upon this one aspect of the period unbalances him a little; his study remains original, learned, fascinating.

Such a study is particularly interesting at a time when 'climates of opinion' are fluctuating once more and our view of the universe is subject to influences comparable in importance with those which were at work in the period of the English Renaissance. Between then and now we have developed an historical sense, and with it a self-awareness, alien to the naïvety of the seventeenth century: we are deeply interested in what is happening to us, to 'our generation', to 'our century'; and, unlike our forefathers, we can see the changes in our own climates of opinion already as a part of history.

Our own experience may teach us to look back on the currents of seventeenth-century thought with some detachment and reserve. For it was then that that kind of inquiry into the nature of the universe which came to be called 'rational' was in the bud, and no hopes for its blossom and its fruits were deemed extravagant. Already 'the sonnes of Adam' were 'as busie as ever he himself was, about the Tree of Knowledge of good and evil, shaking the boughs of it, and scrambling for the fruit'. The tree has spread and blossomed and satisfied the appetites of two centuries, till today not a few are beginning to suspect that its apples are dead-sea fruit, which, if they do not turn to ashes in the mouth, at least fail to satisfy the hunger within.

'In approaching the question of the rejection of scholasticism,' says Mr. Willey, 'it is both our duty and our privilege today to consider the two world views with no antecedent prejudice in favour of the modern.' We cannot be quite as confident as we might have been a hundred years ago that the new knowledge, the new attitude, were pure gain, either for literature or for life. Mr. Willey is helped in his detachment by his own somewhat pragmatic outlook in philosophy. A belief to him is not true, it can be no more than true 'to' him who

[61]

holds it; 'metaphysical beliefs, having their roots in the emotions, are probably incapable of proof or disproof'; the controversies of the seventeenth century have for him therefore a somewhat formal interest, and the passionate convictions, the creeds and the controversies, of the disputants are to him interesting merely as pieces of 'mental behaviour'.

Such a view of history certainly has its advantages. We cannot revivify, we cannot even read, the voluminous controversies of the seventeenth century unless we are possessed of an unusual desire of knowledge for its own sake. We cannot help feeling at times as we explore the writings of this period as if we were observing the inmates of an aquarium, who demand not sympathy but scientific study. Tolerance, impartiality, wide-eyed vigilance will no doubt characterize the work of those who conduct their inquiry in this spirit: one who sees men only as thinkers, and creeds only as specimens, is not likely to be blinded by the mists of any sectarian prejudice. But this attitude is apt to lead to the treatment of men as mere instruments of thought, just as concentration upon the thought of an age is itself apt to turn history into a procession of ideas divorced from events. It tempts us to forget that these strange believers really believed their creeds and often believed things totally inconsistent with them, that they were rooted by innumerable prejudices to the age they lived in, and were rarely conscious of the 'movements' in which we see that they were leaders.

The historian looks back over three hundred years and observes the development of thought, its setbacks, the clashes and the oppositions it encounters, the affinities and alliances of mind with mind, the new territory won by reason, and how reason fortifies and organizes its acquisitions. All this may be true, all this may have happened; the historian's account of it is certainly no fiction, but still it is something less than a full record: the greater part of life is perforce omitted from it. Mr. Willey's seventeenth century is something that never existed, something abstracted from the complex and heterogeneous life actually lived at the time.

To make some such construction is no doubt a historian's business.

But we must beware of accepting it as the picture of an age. And a history of thought, unless its terms and its range are carefully qualified, is above all others apt to be misleading. Our own inquisitive and self-conscious age, an age in which knowledge is rapidly disseminated, popularized, and somehow or other digested, is perhaps an exception. The theory of Relativity has no doubt already influenced the minds of thousands quite unqualified to understand its import; the 'intellectual' is no longer a small and a social category; the 'masses' do not lag so far behind the pioneers of thought as they have done always in the past. Moreover, it is one of the results of that naturalistic outlook which the seventeenth century inaugurated, that the prestige of faith has sunk and the prevalence of a mongrel rationalism has diminished those glaring and unconscious inconsistencies of belief which must perplex the intellectual history of an earlier age. Society today is by comparison accessible, level, homogeneous. It is easy, therefore, for us, as we look back upon what may seem the orderly progress of liberal thought, conquering the provinces of science, of philosophy, of theology, of social life, from Bacon onwards, to forget that the spectacle before our eyes is an historical abstraction, something which never happened quite thus in the world of men.

For a corrective, we must remember a little about human nature, a little of the detailed history of the age in question, of those physical and social trivialities which are the negligible foreground in the intellectual landscape. These things leave doctrine itself, it may be, unaffected; the toothache of a philosopher does not divert his argument. But one need have no very 'materialist' view of history to realize that doctrines can be conveyed only by the written or the printed word; that their discoverers are men with a personal history, whose relations with their contemporaries were governed by innumerable factors unconnected with philosophy, and that the workings of these doctrines were limited and determined by the facilities of publication, the power of ecclesiastical or civic censorship, by the state of education prevailing at the time. Where we deal with anything as complex as society, or as a single human being, to generalize or to simplify is to give only one aspect of the picture.

Of no age is this more obviously true than the seventeenth century,

[63]

when a small minority outstripped their contemporaries in cultivation, when the most enlightened inquirers were the most devout pietists, and the wildest libertarians the most tyrannical in the enforcement of their own discipline. Humanism and Puritanism, in themselves poles apart, the opposing magnets of the age, could be reconciled in a figure like Baxter; and the same man sought to undermine all belief in God and at the same time, above all others in that age, accorded the King an unimpeachable authority in affairs of Church as well as State. If we must choose a metaphor to stand as title for the picture of a century in which a man might be Churchman, soldier, politician, poet and philosopher at once, and subject in each capacity to influences of whose conflict he was unaware, no better word can be found than that chosen by Professor Grierson—'cross-currents'—for his admirable study of the period.

Consider in this period, for instance, the Cambridge Platonists. 'The starting-point of the Cambridge philosophers,' says Mr. Willey, 'was opposition to Hobbes.' Certainly no two men could be as philosophers more radically opposed to each other than Hobbes, the arch-materialist, and Henry More, the apostle of spirit. Yet to one who has in view only the emancipation of thought from the chains of medievalism Hobbes and More will stand side by side, allies of light against darkness. Mr. Willey does full justice to the paradox, and to the more treacherous affinity between More and Descartes. But even the casual reader of the Cambridge Platonists will question whether opposition to Hobbes gave the original impulse to the thought of any of them. Dates alone are enough to invalidate the suggestion that it was, historically, their starting point. 'Ink and paper,' their most serious philosopher declared, 'will never make us Christians'; Christianity for them was a kind of life; and, conversely, it was not the writings but the lives and actions of other men that turned them into philosophers. They could not but range themselves, as thinkers, against a doctrine that denied the very existence of spirit; but intolerance in ecclesiastical administration, bitterness in religious controversy, profligacy and hypocrisy in the life of every day, ink and blood spilt for matters merely temporal and indifferent—these were the things that brought their philosophic movement into being. They

[64]

loathed the doctrine of predestination not as theorists looking for texts to contradict it, as did Milton in his 'De Doctrina Christiana', but because they knew the kind of life that it encouraged.

To understand them, or their contemporaries, fully we must consider not merely the thoughts but the passions of the time, not merely Scholasticism and Platonism, but Puritanism: we must recall the conditions ruling in the Church, at Court, and in the universities: we must remember not merely Descartes, but the Westminster Assembly. Side by side with sermons and with treatises we must read Baxter's 'Reliquiae' and George Fox's 'Journal', and the 'Autobiography' of Lord Herbert as well as his 'De Veritate'. Nor must we neglect the vagaries of individual temperament, and the power of the human mind to accommodate inconsistencies within itself. Man has never shown himself more plainly a 'great amphibium', capable of living in two worlds at once with no consciousness of any conflict, than in the century that produced Sir Thomas Browne. Scepticism was retorted by Glanville (as it had been by Montaigne) upon the Rationalism that engendered it: and a new consciousness of the *impossibilia* of theology gave but a zest to the recital of its *credo*. It was a period with the double head of Janus, looking back and forward at the same time: and only the very clear-sighted were conscious of their ancipitous vision.

All this the historian, so long as he is concerned with doctrine only, is at liberty to forget. Danger begins when he attempts to apply in other spheres conclusions reached by studying thought in abstraction from the world in which these thinkers lived. Mr. Willey believes that a poet cannot swim against the tide of thought, that he cannot write unless his age provides him with a set of beliefs suitable for his purposes. 'The degree of assurance with which serious poetry can be written at any period depends upon the prevailing state of certainty about ultimate issues.' The thought of an age is closely connected therefore with its poetry, and the analysis that Mr. Willey has made of intellectual movements in this period dominates him in his consideration of its literature. The scientific, the naturalistic, view of the universe is, in his view, hostile to the spirit, to religion, to poetry itself. The liberation of the intellect was an advance, but it involved a sacrifice: fact replaced faith, with results fatal to our literature. Hence a sterility, a sense of make-believe, a 'divided sensibility', which lay, heavy as frost, upon English poetry from the days of Dryden till the break of a new dawn with Wordsworth. For it was Wordsworth who, freeing himself alike from the doubts which paralysed the poetic faculty in the transitional period and from the easy certainty that killed it in the age of reason, found a new gospel which was at once a faith for every day and a poetic inspiration: life and poetry for him could be one, as they had been for no poet during the century before him. With passage after passage from 'The Prelude' Mr. Willey illustrates this original and persuasive thesis; and he further claims that, since naturalism had exploded the old mythologies, Wordsworth was forced to create his own poetic scheme, a scheme in which no symbols stood between him and the outer world.

It is true that, when Wordsworth wrote, for a hundred years and more something had been lacking. A realm of possible emotion had been lost to the poet. And lost not only to the poet, but to mankind at large, who cannot help looking for symbols, for something to attract and evoke those associations that can never be generated by scientific statement. As Leslie Stephen pointed out in his *History of English Thought in the Eighteenth Century*, poetry needs the symbolism and the language of religion. A new account of the universe, with new terms and new symbols, kills the old, and only time can bestow upon it a magic property of its own. There is a period when the new outlook has replaced the old but has not yet acquired an inner significance, when the poet who has been taught the secrets of the cyclones and the tides longs, but longs in vain, to have sight of Proteus, to hear old Triton blow his wreathed horn. The old enchanter is dead, and his wand has lost its magic, and as yet no successor has arisen in his stead:

> *The intelligible forms of ancient poets,*
> *The fair humanities of old religion,*
> *The power, the beauty, and the majesty . . .*
> *They live no longer in the faith of reason.*

That is the second purpose of Mr. Willey's survey; and it is here

[66]

that his abstraction from the complex world in which his thinkers lived has led him in more than one respect astray. Having traced the development of 'the faith of reason', he deplores its sterilizing influence on poetry. Its result was, he declares, that poetry could not be written. How was it possible, he asks, that *Paradise Lost*, an epic of the Old Testament, should be written in a rationalizing age?

Such a question could not be asked by one who was not to some degree the victim of his own abstractions. For, though some poets may be today, and may have been in the past, bewildered by the lack of a fundamental certainty, or paralysed in their creative power by their acceptance of a philosophic system from which the imagination is excluded, it is not so with all poets: some still will find matter and a manner of their own. 'Still,' we may misquote, 'the heart doth find a language,' still 'the old instinct' brings back 'the old names' or endows new names with magic: and, just as one who is not a poet will get no good of all the mythologies and all his own most passionate belief, so will the poet create for himself his own symbols and a universe of his own in the face of philosophers to whose arguments he has no answer. He lives not in the abstract world of thought, where a philosophic movement can checkmate his inspiration, but in the world of men, where a thousand cross-currents beat upon his mind and his heart. And while Newton and Hobbes conspire to make it impossible for him to write a line, he may defeat their conspiracy by the simple act of falling in love. We need take but one example from this very age: Shakespeare, than whom none was more deeply shaken in 'assurance' by the New Philosophy, gave it a poet's answer in his tragedies and in his sonnets.

The Essay on Man[1]

'The town is very full of a new poem entitled an Essay on Man, attributed, I think with reason, to a divine.' So one literary man wrote to another in March 1733. The first part of the 'Essay' had just appeared anonymously, and everyone was wondering who wrote it and whether it should be praised. 'I had a hundred things to talk to you of, and among the rest, of the Essay on Man, which I hear so much of. Pray what is your opinion of it? I hear some cry it extremely up; others think it obscure in part.'

It will not surprise those who are acquainted with the manifestations of Pope's candour that he himself should have written both the passages just quoted: nor yet that he should continue 'I give you my thoughts very candidly of it, though I find there is a sort of fashion to set up the author and his piece in opposition to me and my little things.' Every artifice in Pope's whole apparatus of deception had been employed in order to keep the secret of his authorship. His evident preoccupation with the 'Essay' and his concern to free it from the charge of 'infidelity', besides the quality of the poem itself, were indeed enough to put most of his acquaintances on their guard; but while the public praise was all the sweeter because it could not be written off as tribute to an established reputation, the praises of his friends were none the less pleasing because given tentatively, with an uneasy consciousness that the giver might be exalting an unknown rival at the expense of Pope and his 'little things'. Having enjoyed for some months the fruits of this 'innocent deception', Pope put his name to the fourth Epistle, and (in Johnson's phrase) 'claimed the honour of a moral poet'.

That honour did not go for long unchallenged. It was upon the

[1] 1933.

morality, not upon the poetry, that attack was first delivered. For Pope was broaching a subject that had occupied the minds of the reading and the talking world in England, as well as the world of thought, for more than a quarter of a century: Reason and Religion were topics of the hour, theological discussion was not confined to the study, it was the pastime of the coffee-house and the drawing-room. An Essay on Man was sure to find readers in any quarter just as ready to detect infidelity as bathos: readers to whom irreligion was fully as shocking as false taste. It was generally agreed that the Deists and the Free-thinkers were beneath the contempt of respectable men; yet respectable men, from Swift and Berkeley downwards, spent much of their time in exposing the impiety of a merely 'natural' religion. The 'Essay', an undisguised panegyric of Reason which contained hardly a single unequivocal reference to the Christian faith, could not fail to bring its author, though he was a professed Catholic, into some suspicion. Indeed, to own Bolingbroke as 'master of the poet and the song' was to invite calumny; and it did not take long for the tale to get about that the 'Essay' was nothing more than Pope's translation of a prose-sketch in which Bolingbroke had outlined his own atheistic system. In short, there was 'a general alarm about its fatalism and deistical tendency'. It is well known how, when the attack was concentrated by de Crousaz, Warburton leaped to its defence and discovered in it a thousand proofs of orthodoxy never intended by its author: how Pope adopted him as an expositor, and he thus managed to scrape not merely an acquaintance but an undying friendship with the poet.

The attack and the reply were both so obviously misconceived that to a later generation the whole affair must seem a mere skiomachy. To represent the 'Essay on Man' as a systematic exposition hostile to revealed religion is to do too much honour to its argument; to look in it for proof or disproof of Pope's personal piety is to take it for something other than it is. Nothing was farther from Pope's intention, nothing indeed was less within his power, than a sustained piece of reasoning on the Deist side. On the other hand, his Essay was not intended as an expression of personal devotion or a panegyric of the Christian faith. Young, when he entreated Pope to do for Revelation what he had done for Reason, showed an understanding of the limited purpose of the 'Essay' which was not shared by a majority either of those who attacked or of those who defended it. As Warton records, Pope 'had inserted an address to Jesus Christ in the Essay on Man, which he omitted at the instance of Bishop Berkeley, because the Christian religion did not come within the compass of his plan'; his plan could exclude such an apostrophe in favour of an address to Bolingbroke, the apostle of Reason, without any loss of piety, for Reason and Revelation were complementary, not antagonistic.

The misunderstandings on either side would have been impossible had it not been for the mists of unreality that overhung the battle-field on which Pope's contemporaries were engaged. The fight is not so much between shadows as between blindfolded men. For a battle between shadows is a battle, though to us the encounter may seem unsubstantial; the combatants engage, *belli simulacra cientes*, they deal blows, they suffer wonds, they fall; there is victory, there is defeat. Such was the warfare waged by the religious disputants of Elizabethan and of Stuart times; however little the issues between them mean to us, those issues were defined, and to them meant everything. They understood each other, and their blows went home. But the figures of eighteenth-century controversy, though they have stepped quite clear of the mist of the Middle Ages, and are to us in many ways familiar and intelligible men, seem to be occupied in a warfare that is far less real. They go through the motions of attack and defence, but what is it that is at stake? The issues between them are never patent even to the combatants themselves; they strike wildly in the air, their blows never engage.

The Deistic and the Freethinking controversies were alike involved in this obscurity; the heterodox never fought openly under the standard of rebellion, and their adversaries were content to behave as if rebellion was impossible. Those who exalted Reason stopped short of claiming that Reason was inconsistent with a belief in the Christian revelation: those who explained away miracles were careful to say that Christianity did not depend upon such support: those who urged that the Bible, with its 30,000 variant readings, must stand, like any other ancient book, the scrutiny of textual critics, did not suggest that its authority might be thus impaired.

They set forth the premises and left their adversaries to draw the conclusions. When those conclusions were drawn they recoiled with indignation; and it is difficult to know whether their indignation was genuine or feigned. 'To what purpose should I study here or elsewhere' asks Toland, 'were I an atheist or a deist, for one of the two you take me to be? or in what a condition to mention virtue, if I believed there was no God?'

The orthodox, on the other hand, refused to face, even to recognize, the issues involved. Their answer to the upholders of Natural Religion was that Christianity was the most natural of religions, to the champions of Reason that Christianity was reasonableness itself. 'That which is the Demonstration of our Faith,' wrote Zachary Pearce, 'can never be the Foundation of Their Infidelity.' It was in this spirit that Bentley answered Collins's 'Discourse of Freethinking':

' 'Tis plain, a Man that is born in a Christian Country, if he is a Just and Good Man, has no interest to wish that Religion false. . . . No foreign Religion, much less the Atheistic Scheme, threaten him with any danger; should he be here in an Error. He's as safe, as those that differ from him, were he really in the wrong. But then if it be true; what glorious Promises and Rewards, not superior only to other Schemes but beyond all Human wishes?'

Christianity, in short, is to be recommended as a trustee investment. It is not only safe, it is also easy; for, he continues, 'the speculative Doctrines in it (which affect the main chance) are very few and easy. If his Education has enabled him for't, he'l examin Them and the whole grounds of Faith, and find them true to his satisfaction and comfort'. A man who could reason thus was not the man to argue with an atheist; he could not believe that an atheist existed; to him those who did not accept the articles of Christian belief were either madmen or rogues or dunces, and the way to meet them was not with argument but with abuse.

In such an atmosphere as this flourished the controversy to which the 'Essay' was deemed to be a contribution; by the end of the century it was forgotten, not simply because it was over, but because it never had been real.

Today it is not as philosophy but as poetry that the 'Essay' is likely to be criticized. And in judging it as poetry its detractors may insist against it as a fault, not that it is bad philosophy, but that it tries to be philosophy at all. For if, as we are told today, the reasoning mind is an intruder in the realm of poetry and poetic varies in inverse proportion to intellectual content, the very possibility of philosophical poetry must be called in question. Faced with this deep aesthetic problem, the common reader may be content to reflect that though good reasoning is something very different from good poetry and the beauty of the one very different from the beauty of the other, though reasoning, good or bad, and poetry rarely exist together, and though to be at once a philosopher and a poet is to achieve the rarest of combinations, none the less, the poetic thrill (even if, as several observers assure us, it is of a nature purely physical) comes sometimes with its greatest force when charged with intellectual significance: the reasoning mind often plays no small part in generating it. *Nil igitur mors est :* how much of the poetic force of those passionate words is owed to *igitur* and its implications! What would not the purple passages from the *De Rerum Natura* suffer if abstracted from their setting, where they have behind them the whole force of the poem and its argument? Philosophical poetry, though rare, is possible. But Pope did not achieve it.

Of the reasons for his failure the most obvious has been indicated in discussing his philosophy. The poem does not present a system. It is 'a mighty maze of walks without a plan'; so it remains, for all Warburton's efforts to prove the contrary and for all the surreptitious patches and amendments introduced into it by its author. The very ease with which by changing a couple of words—'a mighty maze *but not* without a plan'—he could transform the nature of his subject is some indication of the carelessness with which the poem was constructed. The fine passages in it, therefore, and fine passages there are in plenty, owe little to their context: its beauties are not strung together by any single thread of serious thought running through and colouring the texture of the whole.

The absence of system, though it prevents the Essay from being a philosophical poem in the highest sense, does not explain why it fails altogether to deserve that name; for even the piecemeal presentment of a crude philosophy may be poetically moving in a way in

which the Essay is not. Those who have felt, even as it were in fragments, a sense of the last and largest problems of human life, those
who have assumed even for a moment an attitude determined by
their consciousness of the relations between an inner and an outer
world, those who have caught a glimpse, whether in the temple or in
the tavern, of the universe as a whole, all these may write something
—however inadequate their attitude, however confused their
representation of it—that will move us with a force akin to that of
poetry truly philosophical. Of this truth both Wordsworth and
Omar Khayyam, in all their extreme dissimilarity, are alike examples.
In the 'Essay on Man' Pope, like these two authors, approaches
without the aid of powerful or continuous thought the ultimate
problems of existence. If he does not move us as they do, it is partly
on account of the attitude he has chosen to adopt, partly on account
of the spirit in which he adopts it.

'Sheer optimism,' said Leslie Stephen, 'is the least vigorous of
beliefs.' It is also the least invigorating; it starves the emotions. To
one who believes that 'whatever is, is right' experience is reduced to
a uniformity duller even than despair. Even he who believes that
man will go down into the pit and all his works must perish, and he
who sees human life as the plaything of some malignant deity, or all
existence as an 'unearthly ballet' of abstractions, may well feel to the
full the hopeless vanity of human effort and the poignancy of human
aspiration; and the attitude of mind in which such thinkers confront
their destiny may well arouse in those who contemplate it deep
emotion. But optimism when faced with experience that contradicts
its tenets is at a loss. The wisdom that teaches us not to weep cannot
dry our tears, still less can it draw them forth: the poetry in which it
is expounded can hardly be endowed with emotional power:

> *Wants, frailties, passions closer still ally*
> *The common int'rest or endear the tie.*
> *To these we owe true friendship, love sincere,*
> *Each home-felt joy that life inherits here;*
> *Yet from the same we learn in its decline*
> *Those joys, those loves, those int'rests to resign;*
> *Taught half by reason, half by mere decay,*

The Essay on Man

To welcome death, and calmly pass away . . .
The learn'd is happy nature to explore,
The fool is happy that he knows no more,
The rich is happy in the plenty giv'n,
The poor contents him with the care of heav'n.

It is hard to see here the sources of the tears of things, and a poet who would elicit them from such a philosophy would need the rod of Moses.

Not only, however, was Pope's philosophical creed (in so far as he had one) hostile to poetry; the spirit in which he held it was calculated to sterilize emotion. He has no sense, it seems, of the awfulness of the problems with which he deals. In this he was a victim of the conditions of his age. When the grand problems of human destiny are topics of common debate, they lose their grandeur; when the man in the street is a philosopher, philosophy becomes debased. All but the most distinguished minds of the time treated abstractions with a nonchalance that arose from undue familiarity. 'In the course of his lectures,' wrote an undergraduate of Magdalen, recalling a course in Divinity at Oxford later in the century, 'he arrived at the momentous question πόθεν τὸ κακόν; Why does not God prevent the existence of evil ? . . . I forget the solution of the difficulty adopted by the Regius Professor. I remember only the monotonous drawl and air of *pococuranteism* and indifference with which it was stated; amounting almost to hebetude.'

Pope was a little like the Regius Professor. When he tells us that God sees with equal eyes 'now a bubble burst and now a world', we feel that he shares the divine indifference; even when he splendidly calls man 'the glory, jest and riddle of the world' we feel that he himself is hardly impressed or amused or perplexed by the phenomenon. In this he probably did himself less than justice, but the impression remains, and it is intensified by contrast when we turn to Sir John Davies, whose *Nosce Teipsum* Pope must, it seems, have had in mind at some points of the 'Essay':

> *I know my life's a paine and but a span.*
> *I know my sense is mockt with everything;*
> *And to conclude, I know myselfe a man,*
> *Which is a proud, and yet a wretched thing.*

[74]

The Essay on Man

There is no doubting the personal sincerity of either poet; but Davies alone writes as if he felt the grandeur and abasement of the human lot, and his feeling is intimately connected with his philosophic thought.

The contrast recurs where the two poets treat of human ignorance. 'Go, wondrous creature!' writes Pope, in an eloquent passage too long to quote in full—

> *Mount where Science guides—*
> *Go, measure earth, weigh air, and state the tides;*
> *Instruct the planets in what orbs to run,*
> *Correct old Time, and regulate the Sun . . .*
> *Go, teach Eternal Wisdom how to rule—*
> *Then drop into thyself, and be a fool!*

The eloquence is moving, but it does not move us, as does Davies, to the humility that the poet preaches:

> *We seeke to know the moving of each spheare,*
> *And the strange cause of th' ebs and flouds of Nile:*
> *But of that clocke within our breasts we beare,*
> *The subtill motions we forget the while.*

> *We that acquaint our selves with every* Zoane,
> *And passe both* Tropikes *and behold the* Poles,
> *When we come home are to our selves unknown,*
> *And unacquainted still with our owne* soules.

Pope was mistaken, one must conclude, in attempting to expound in verse a philosophy he did not understand and one that did not move him deeply—a philosophy, moreover, that was essentially prosaic. The poem that he wrote can be read with great enjoyment, but it is not the best he can give us: he was a man capable of feeling deep emotion, and a poet capable of arousing it, and he is at his greatest when he lives in what he writes. His pre-eminent passions were not of the tender kind, and it is as a satirist that he excels. In the 'Essay' itself from time to time he comes to life, and it is when the satirist is speaking; we have only to compare the virtuosity of

[75]

The Essay on Man

Why has not man a microscopic eye?
For this plain reason: Man is not a fly—

with such a line as this

All sly, slow things with circumspective eyes—

to see where his true talent lay: in such passages as the following, the philosopher forgets himself, to his infinite advantage, in the satirist:

Stuck o'er with titles and hung round with strings,
That thou may'st be by kings, or whores of kings,
The richest blood, right-honourably old,
Down from Lucretia to Lucretia roll'd,
May swell thy heart and gallop in thy breast
Without one dash of usher or of priest . . .
But by your fathers' worth if yours you rate
Count me those only who were good and great.
What can ennoble sots, or slaves, or cowards?
Alas! not all the blood of all the Howards.

That passage (which he toned down for publication in the 'Essay') attests his genius and its true scope: reading it, we are impelled immediately to turn to his Satires and Epistles; there we shall find the poet interested and at home, not wandering in the 'mighty maze' with his eye on an abstraction; and there the quality of his work, fine poetry if anything deserves the name, will convince us that men, and not Man, were his proper study.

Dr. Johnson's Letters[1]

Perhaps the subtlest form of literary partnership is the relation that subsists between a biographer and his subject—a collaboration, indeed, we may rightly call it, for each, the living man and the dead, may be said in some sense to work upon the other. As the tyrant in the old epic condemned the prisoners he took in battle to be bound, each of them, to the corpse of a dead comrade, so the biographer—and the same is true, more or less, of every serious student of past lives—is condemned to the closest union with his dead subject, to share his world, to see with his eyes, to 'partake' (like Southey's scholar) his 'hopes and fears', and to become if not his friend at least his intimate companion.

To one who embarks in this spirit upon the study of a life, that life will come to be measured not in epochs or periods, not in years or even months, but (if the evidence is sufficient) in days and hours; he will see it as a series of Mondays, Tuesdays and Wednesdays, with an eye open not only to changes of party and changes of opinion but to changes in the weather and changes of address. The aim of such an intimate association is, of course, that the living should bring to life the dead; but the undertaking is not without its dangers: sometimes the detailed past lays a mortifying hand upon the present, and the unfortunate immortals are buried in tomes truly sepulchral, by devotees who seem themselves to have lost the breath of life. Not a few such biographical cenotaphs exist in our literature, reminding us of the peril that besets the path of writers who set out to seek the living among the dead.

Few scholars can have lived longer or more intimately with the

[1] A review of *The Letters of Samuel Johnson* edited by R. W. Chapman, 1953.

subject of their study than has Dr. Chapman, none has escaped more completely the deadening touch of pedantry; he has been in close communion with Samuel Johnson for more than a quarter of a century, and he not only knows the background of Johnson's life in its minutest detail, but breathes its very air. We are now presented with the fruit of this intimate association, not, indeed, in the shape of a biography; Dr. Chapman has chosen another method of bringing Dr. Johnson to life: he has set out to do for Johnson's letters what Dr. Powell did for Boswell's *Life*: to provide an edition which shall be, humanly speaking, definitive and final. Both have benefited from the pioneering work of Birkbeck Hill, but Dr. Powell more than Dr. Chapman: Hill's edition of the *Life* needed to be re-edited, but his edition of the *Letters* had to be discarded and a new work put in its place.

A few figures will suffice to show the magnitude of Dr. Chapman's undertaking. Four years after Johnson's death, Mrs. Piozzi printed some 350 of his letters; to these, in the *Life*, published three years later, Boswell added about as many more. Almost exactly a century after the publication of the *Life*, Birkbeck Hill edited the first comprehensive collection of Johnson's correspondence, numbering 1,043 letters—a figure which may mislead, since this numeration includes letters printed by Boswell in the *Life*, the text of which Hill excluded from his edition. Dr. Chapman has added to Hill's total 472 letters which till now have been unpublished or uncollected, printing in full —and for the first time in texts 'as accurate and complete as the evidence allows'—the letters hitherto left embedded in the *Life*. Moreover, he gives us about 100 unpublished letters of Mrs. Thrale. This vast collection, forming (as he says) 'in essentials the first edition of Johnson's letters as a whole', fills some 1,500 pages, divided into three volumes adorned with facsimiles of Johnson's autograph and printed with a sober elegance characteristic of the Clarendon Press.

'My prime ambition,' says Dr. Chapman, 'has been to furnish an accurate text,' and his text is without doubt more correct, as it is more complete, than any of its predecessors. His unrivalled knowledge of Johnson's hand and his flair for a right reading have aided him both in his 'diligent scrutiny of originals and in those cases where he had to depend upon copies, whether in manuscript or in print. How strict is his attention to *minutiae* and how intelligent are the purposes it serves may be gauged from the following introductory statement of his aims:

'I have aimed at reproducing my manuscripts as closely as typography admits. . . .

'In one not unimportant point I have deserted my originals. Johnson, like others of his time, normally "displayed" his conclusions, which at their most elaborate might, if space allowed, run to five or six lines. The motive of this was partly deference, but it was partly aesthetic. Now when letters are printed consecutively this display is extravagant, and not merely ceases to be decorative but becomes an offence to the eye. I have therefore telescoped the subscriptions throughout.

'I have preserved Johnson's occasional inadvertences, such as the omission or repetition of small words, partly because they furnish some indication of his state of health or his state of mind, partly because they show the sort of error to which he was prone and may therefore help us in judging the text of those letters of which the originals are lost.'

Shrewdness and aesthetic sensibility determine Dr. Chapman's decision on what may seem merely pedantic questions; his notes, the part of such a work which is perhaps the most difficult to execute satisfactorily, are marvellously condensed and challengingly allusive; they presuppose an alert and educated reader. They are the product of a rigid self-discipline: Dr. Chapman never shirks, and is never afraid to confess, a difficulty; he never annotates for the sake of annotation or to display his learning; his aim is always, and only, to elucidate.

Dr. Chapman is able to lighten his commentary by reason of the fullness of his indexes, which are the most remarkable feature of this edition. He has already shown us, in his edition of Jane Austen's letters, how full a flood of light can be thrown upon the whole *milieu* of a correspondence, upon the world in which its author lived, by indexes imaginatively planned and intelligently composed. The indexes to the present work (which occupy some 150 pages) fulfil several of the purposes of a commentary and present in convenient synoptic form material for a portrait of Johnson himself or a conversation-piece of Johnson among his friends. A list of the indexes will give some idea of their scope, but quotation is necessary in order to do justice to their quality. They are seven in number: (i) Samuel Johnson ('I have in this index tried to classify what may be called the autobiographical elements in the letters under the heads of Books, Character, Charities, Conversation, Correspondence, Domesticity, The Fashionable World, Friends and Acquaintances, Godchildren, Habitations, Health and Spirits, Hobbies, Languages, Livelihood, Loneliness, Personal Appearance, Politics, Quarrels, Reading and Writing, Religion, University Honours'); (ii) Persons; (iii) Authors and Books; (iv) Places; (v) Subjects ('Johnson's opinions on general topics are here grouped under the headings Americans, Architecture, Balloons, Building, Clubs, Death and Immortality . . . Religion, Scots, Sea and Ships, Theatre, Things, Household Concerns, &c., Transport, Travel, Youth'); (vi) Johnson's Works; (vii) Johnson's English.

With what sensitive art these lists are compiled may be judged from an introductory note to the Index of Persons: 'A student of any of J.'s intimacies will naturally turn first to his letters to the person concerned. For that reason facts and opinions about A.B. in letters to A.B. are more lightly indexed than facts and opinions about A.B. in letters to others.' Something of their fascination may be gathered from a selection of the references that the editor groups chronologically (each with date, and letter-number, here omitted) under the heading 'Character' in Index I:

'(1) *Self-examination.* "I go wrong in opposition to conviction"; "I ought to do many things which I do not"; "too apt to be negligent"; "a pang for every moment that any human being has by my peevishness or obstinacy spent in uneasiness"; "have hitherto lived without the concurrence of my own judgement"; "corroded with vain and idle discontent"; "a life of which I do not like the review"; "three score and four years in which little has been done . . . a life diversified by misery"; "any good of myself I am not very easy to believe"; "I have through my whole progress of authorship honestly endeavoured to teach the right, though I have not been sufficiently diligent to practise it"; "from the retrospect of life . . . I shrink with multiplicity of horrour . . . I look forward with less pain."

'(2) *Self-portraiture*. I remark that J. hardly mentions his mental powers except his memory; on his genius and learning he is silent. "A retired and uncourtly scholar"; "I think it impossible that I should have suffered such a total obliteration, from my mind, of anything that was ever there"; "a bad manager in a crowd"; "I fret at your forgetfulness as I do at my own"; "as I have not the decrepitude I have not the callousness of old age"; "I am afraid that I bear the weight of time with unseemly impatience"; "I love a little secret history"; "the town is my element".'

The composition of such a list as this is anything but mechanical; a like art has gone to the construction of the numerous appendices and the rest of the critical apparatus of this edition: Dr. Chapman so articulates the dry bones of biography as to give them a life of their own.

What of the portrait that emerges from this vast mass of personal material? Dr. Chapman suggests that he may justly repeat the claim made on Boswell's title-page:

> quo fit ut *omnis*
> votiva pateat veluti depicta tabella
> vita senis.

In one sense, that claim cannot be made good—unless indeed we stress the word *senis*: the whole of Johnson's life is not depicted for us by his letters, any more than it is by the portraits drawn of him by other hands: Reynolds, Opie, Nollekens show us the Doctor in his maturity or his old age; he was fifty and more when Boswell and Mrs. Thrale first came to know him; and it is inevitable that he should live for the eye and ear of posterity as one who is well past the meridian of life. We no more think of him as Tetty's husband, or as the awkward young usher of Market Bosworth, than we think of Miss Burney as the old lady of eighty that Mme. D'Arblay grew to be. The *Letters* do little to extend this restricted angle of vision: nine-tenths of those

F   [81]

that survive were written during the last twenty years, two-thirds during the last decade, of Johnson's life: it is to the *vita senis* that they belong. That phase of his life, however, they illumine completely in both its external and its internal aspects.

For its external aspect: the *Letters* reveal even more fully than the *Life* the series of everyday accidents and avocations—'the business of common life'—of which, according to Johnson himself, human existence is predominantly composed. We see him surrounded by admirers, *protégés*, dependants; busy with proof-sheets, dedications, engagements to dine, arrangements for travel; occupied with all the paraphernalia to which Dr. Chapman's indexes provide a comprehensive guide—and, increasingly, in correspondence with his physicians. Innumerable are the letters to Brocklesby about squills and Heberden about rhubarb, to Lawrence about emetick tartar and Hunter about ipecacuanha; indeed, we might well tire of hearing how Mudge recommended clysters and what Pott said of Sarcopheles, did we not remember that such touches, omitted by Boswell and Mrs. Piozzi as beneath the notice of polite readers, bring home to us as nothing else the conditions of a life which through its whole course was rendered radically wretched by disease and by the apprehension of it.

It is not, however, for the light they shed on the external aspects of Johnson, but for their revelation of his character and mind, that the letters are chiefly to be valued. Here indeed they supplement the less balanced portraits presented by other sources. The traditional image of Johnson, a figure crudely 'Johnsonian', compounded of roast beef and common sense, the Great Bear of English letters, growling out contradictions from a tavern chair, has given place in the minds of modern readers to a very different Johnson, melancholy, introspective, neurotic, lonely in the midst of company, tortured by a sense of sin and haunted by the fear of death. Each picture has a foundation of truth, but each is at best one-sided; it is the combination in him of such apparently inconsistent personalities that makes Johnson so fascinating a figure; and his letters reveal this combination more fully than do any other documents. They show us not only Johnson among his companions of the club, not only the solitary Johnson of the *Prayers and Meditations*, but Johnson in all the varied relations of everyday life.

The literary dictator puts in an occasional appearance: the 'celebrated letter' to Chesterfield and the scarcely less celebrated letter to Macpherson take their appropriate places; and we see flashes, in epistolary form, of the winged (and barbed) words that Boswell pinned to his page: 'I hoped'—he writes to Boswell, who had become so troubled by reading Monboddo and Kames on 'the perplexing question of Liberty and Necessity' that he 'went out into the wood and groaned'—'I hoped you had got rid of all this hypocrisy of misery. What have you to do with Liberty and Necessity? Or what more than to hold your tongue about it?' At times the accents of the tavern oracle are audible:

'The fate of the balloon I do not much lament. To make new balloons is to repeat the jest again. We now know a method of mounting into the air, and I think, are not likely to know more.'

That is simply Johnson's speaking voice; he never attempted to cultivate letter-writing as an art; he did not even count it, as did Pope and Gray, Cowper and Horace Walpole, a pleasing occupation: 'I find myself very unwilling,' he tells Dr. Taylor, 'to take up a pen only to tell my friends that I am well.' Again:

'I love to see my friends, to hear from them, to talk to them, and to talk of them; but it is not without a considerable effort of resolution that I prevail upon myself to write. I would not, however, gratify my own indolence by the omission of any important duty, or any office of real kindness.'

It was when the 'offices of kindness' called for it that Johnson gave of himself to his correspondents, and the self that he gave them was his best. The tyrant of Fleet Street, whose utterance made strangers tremble and exposed anonymous clergymen to ridicule, showed, as a correspondent, a wonderful adaptability. He contrived—it was a gift rather of the heart than of the head—to accommodate himself, and to shape his letters, to the characters and needs of their recipients. It was to Boswell, in Dr. Chapman's opinion, that he wrote the most interesting of his letters; his letters to Mrs. Thrale, 'though they are never patronizing, are limited by her power of appreciation. On the other hand they are enriched by her feminine intuitions, which permitted an allusiveness that would have been out of keeping if addressed to a Boswell or a Langton'. Whoever his correspondent, Johnson's letters are, almost all of them, personal in a double sense: he is not so carried away by his subject as to forget either himself or the person to whom he is writing. Indeed, his subject-matter does not often conduce to such forgetfulness, for he touches but little on the affairs of the literary and political world around him, and concerns himself for the most part with matters immediately to hand. Then he distils wisdom, not the impersonal, copy-book wisdom of *The Rambler* or *Rasselas* but wisdom born directly of his own experience and designed to meet the case before him. So he writes to the youthful George Strahan, who feared that he had given offence to his mentor:

'I love you, and hope to love you long. You have hitherto done nothing to diminish my goodwill, and though you had done much more than you have supposed imputed to you my goodwill would not have been diminished.

'I write thus largely on this suspicion which you have suffered to enter your mind, because in youth we are apt to be too rigorous in our expectations, and to suppose that the duties of life are to be performed with unfailing exactness and regularity, but in our progress through life we are forced to abate much of our demands, and to take friends such as we can find them, not as we would make them.'

For the stolid Dr. Taylor, in his matrimonial difficulties, he prepares a suitable mixture of solemnity and sense:

'The happiness of conjugal life cannot be ascertained or secured either by sense or by virtue, and therefore its miseries may be numbered among those evils which we cannot prevent and must only labour to endure with patience, and palliate with judgement. If your condition is known I should think it best to come from the place, that you may not be a gazing stock to idle people who have nobody but you to talk of.'

Touching is his encouragement of Bennet Langton in his care for his brothers and sisters ('I who have no sisters and brothers look with some degree of innocent envy on those who may be said to be born to be friends'); and his approval of Boswell's good intentions is accompanied by a warning that comes evidently from the heart: 'Your resolution to obey your father I entirely approve; but do not accustom yourself to enchain your volatility by vows: they will some time leave a thorn in your mind which you will, perhaps, never be able to extract or eject.'

He could respond to great occasions; death called forth some of his most memorable letters; and perhaps the most moving of them all was occasioned by the death of a friendship—his friendship with Mrs. Thrale. Dignified yet passionate, passionate to the point of poetry, was the letter in which he passed his considered judgment on her impending marriage—a letter atoning for the harsh outburst with which, a few days earlier, he had greeted the disastrous news:

'What you have done, however I may lament it, I have no pretence to resent, as it has not been injurious to me. I therefore breathe out one sigh more of tenderness perhaps useless, but at least sincere.

'I wish that God may grant you every blessing, that you may be happy in this world for its short continuance, and eternally happy in a better state. And whatever I can contribute to your happiness, I am very ready to repay for that kindness which soothed twenty years of a life radically wretched. . . .

'When Queen Mary took the resolution of sheltering herself in England, the Archbishop of St. Andrew's attempting to dissuade her, attended on her journey and when they came to the irremediable stream that separated the two kingdoms, walked by her side into the water, in the middle of which he seized her bridle, and with earnestness proportioned to her danger and his own affection, pressed her to return. The Queen went forward. If the parallel reaches thus far; may it go no further. The tears stand in my eyes.'

'Radically wretched': it was his own experience of unhappiness that made Johnson so wise a minister to the unhappiness of others. From almost the earliest years of which his surviving letters contain a record, they give us intermittent glimpses into the dark world of his melancholy: the fear of death, the fear of disease, the fear of insanity (there is a newly published exchange of letters with Mrs.

Thrale which suggests that he sometimes abandoned himself in good earnest to his *insanae cogitationes*, and that in this matter she was his helper and confidante), a sense of his own unworthiness before his Maker—all these were spectres that never ceased to haunt him, and from time to time we come upon a letter which is simply a *cri de coeur*, uttered from the depths of an unfathomable abyss. It was from such an abyss that he wrote to Lucy Porter, a few days after his mother's death:

'I am not able to determine anything. My grief makes me afraid to be alone. Write to me dear child—'

and to Taylor shortly after the death of Anna Williams:

'O, my friend, the approach of death is very dreadful. I am afraid to think on that which I know I cannot avoid. It is vain to look round and round for help which cannot be had. Yet we hope and hope, and fancy that he who has lived today may live tomorrow. But let us learn to derive our hope only from God.

'In the meantime, let us be kind to one another. I have no friend now living but you and Mr. Hector that was the friend of my youth.'

Death had indeed for him a double terror: it not only threatened his own head, but took away the main comfort of his life, his friends. Increasingly alone, weighed down by a complication of ills, he took up his pen more and more often, not (indeed!) 'only to tell his friends that he was well', but because in his darkening solitude converse with friends was his one remaining solace, and the post afforded the only practicable means of communicating with them. In the last year of his life his letters become more and more frequent; often they are short and simple, and sometimes so trivial that one might think them scarcely worth the sending—till one sees that they were written almost in desperation, simply to elicit the comfort of an answer. The closing scene is certainly a sad one, fit subject for the sombre genius of Rembrandt—the Death of the Lion, there among the shadows in Bolt Court. And yet the final impression we retain is not merely one of suffering: something endures, something emerges, something triumphs, and it is something that was with him the whole length of his life; it colours every page of his correspondence, it is what made him loved and what made him feared—an unfailing current of moral force and moral beauty, flowing, along a channel of natural piety, directly from the strength and the simplicity of his head and of his heart.

Soon after Johnson's death, Dr. Parr, wisely deferring to Boswell, condensed the tomes of a projected biography into the ten lines of an epitaph which may be read today on his memorial statue in St. Paul's. Not all its phrases won the approval of Johnson's friends, but on one all of them must have been agreed: *magister verae virtutis.* In their eyes, no doubt, and in the world's he had earned that title by his published didactic writings; we—who, as Macaulay pointed out, know him more intimately than ever he was known to his contemporaries—may well reflect, when we read his letters to the circle of his friends, that to them he taught 'true virtue' even more effectually by example than he taught it by precept to the world at large.

Jane Austen and Sydney Smith[1]

It is dangerous to attempt to identify the creations of a novelist with persons who actually existed, and Jane Austen's characters afford no exception to this rule. 'I am too proud of my gentlemen,' she is said to have declared, 'to admit that they were only Mr. A, or Colonel B.' This does not, however, mean that, in the creation of character, she did not take hints from the circle of her friends and acquaintances, and in depicting the social scene she certainly stuck close to facts.[2] No reader of *Northanger Abbey* can doubt that its pictures of life in Bath are founded on the writer's own experience, and it is the purpose of this note to suggest that one of its characters may have been put into her mind by a person whom she met there.

Northanger Abbey, first published in 1818, some six months after its author's death, had existed in manuscript for many years. In her own 'Advertisement' to the novel she told her readers: 'This little work was finished in the year 1803, and intended for immediate publication. . . . The public are entreated to bear in mind that thirteen years have passed since it was finished, many more since it was begun, and that during that period places, manners, books, and opinions have undergone considerable changes.' For the period when the book was begun we have the testimony of her family: 'During the first half of 1798, Jane, fresh from her late visit to Bath, was able to devote some happy months of unbroken leisure to writing the first

---

[1] 1954.
[2] For a full discussion of this subject, see Chapter VIII, 'Fact and Fiction', of Dr. R. W. Chapman's *Jane Austen : Facts and Problems*, Clarendon Press, 1948.

draft of the book known to us as *Northanger Abbey*.'¹ How often
Jane Austen, then twenty-two years of age, had already visited Bath
it is not possible to say. She was living with her parents at Steventon,
but she had relations in Bath whom it is to be supposed that she
visited not infrequently in the 1790s.² The visit that the authors of
the *Life and Letters* particularly refer to evidently began in November
1797. They tell us:

'In November of this same year Mrs. Austen, whose health was
not good, determined to go to Bath with her daughters. . . . Mrs.
Austen's brother, Mr. Leigh Perrot, was a regular visitor to Bath,
and there is every reason to suppose that Jane had already visited the
Leigh Perrots or the Coopers, or both, at this still fashionable resort.
. . . Owing to the absence of contemporary letters our knowledge of
her stay there in 1797 is chiefly derived from reminiscences in later
correspondence. Thus in May 1799, when visiting Bath again, Jane
remarks that it rained almost all the way from Devizes, "and our first
view of Bath has been just as gloomy as it was last November twelve-
month". . . . The Austens [they add] probably stayed with the Perrots at their house, No. 1, Paragon Buildings.'³

There seems to be no means of ascertaining exactly how long the
Austens stayed at Bath on this occasion. No letter written by Jane
during this period survives; but her cousin, Elizabeth de Feuillide,
'mentions on December 11 that she had heard very lately from Jane

---

¹ *Jane Austen, her Life and Letters*, by W. and R. A. Austen Leigh, John
Murray, 1913, p. 108, Cassandra, in a *memorandum* quoted (not quite
correctly) on p. 96 of the *Life and Letters*, attributes the writing of
Northanger Abbey to '1798 and 1799'.

² See J. E. Austen Leigh's *Memoir of Jane Austen*, ed. R. W. Chapman,
Clarendon Press, 1926, p. 24: 'The family lived in close intimacy with two
cousins, Edward and Jane Cooper, the children of Mrs. Austen's eldest
sister, and Dr. Cooper, the vicar of Sonning, near Reading. The Coopers
lived for some years at Bath, which seems to have been much frequented
in those days by clergymen retiring from work. I believe that Cassandra
and Jane sometimes visited them there, and that Jane thus acquired the
intimate knowledge of the topography and customs of Bath, which
enabled her to write *Northanger Abbey* long before she resided there herself.'

³ In a letter written on 8 April 1805, also from Bath, Jane again refers to
this visit, dating it '7 years and 4 months ago'—*i.e.*, December 1797 (*Jane
Austen's Letters*, ed. R. W. Chapman, Clarendon Press, 1932, p. 148).

"who is still at Bath with her mother and sister",' and the authors of the *Life and Letters* speak of the party as 'returning home for Christmas'.[1]

It does not seem unreasonable to suggest that Jane Austen sat down to compose the opening chapters of *Northanger Abbey* in the early months of 1798 with recollections of this visit to Bath fresh in her mind, and that, in creating the characters who appear in those chapters, she took hints from persons whom she had actually met while she was there. The most vivid and remarkable of these characters is surely the Reverend Henry Tilney, the young clergyman whom she describes (in Chapter III) as follows: 'He seemed to be about four or five and twenty, was rather tall, had a pleasing countenance, a very intelligent and lively eye, and, if not quite handsome, was very near it.' Readers of Jane Austen will not need to be reminded of the 'fluency and spirit' of his talk and the 'archness and pleasantry in his manner'; but one or two examples of it may be given here:

'I consider a country-dance as an emblem of marriage. Fidelity and complaisance are the principal duties of both; and those men who do not chuse to dance or marry themselves have no business with the partners or wives of their neighbours.' (Oxford ed., p. 76.)

'That little boys and girls should be tormented . . . is what no one at all acquainted with human nature in a civilized state can deny; but in behalf of our most distinguished historians, I must observe, that they might well be offended at being supposed to have no higher aim; and that by their method and style, they are perfectly well qualified to torment readers of the most advanced reason and mature time of life.' (Oxford ed., p. 109.)

'You talked of expected horrors in London—and instead of instantly conceiving, as any rational creature would have done, that such words could relate only to a circulating library, she immediately pictured to herself a mob of three thousand men assembling in St. George's Fields; the Bank attacked, the Tower threatened, the streets of London flowing with blood, a detachment of the 12th Light

[1] P. 106. Was Jane's birthday (16 December) celebrated by her at Bath or at Steventon?

Dragoons (the hopes of the nation) called up from Northampton to quell the insurgents, and the gallant Capt. Frederick Tilney, in the moment of charging at the head of his troop, knocked off his horse by a brickbat from an upper window. Forgive her stupidity. The fears of the sister have added to the weakness of the woman; but she is by no means a simpleton in general.' (Oxford ed., p. 113.)

'I think very highly of the understanding of all the women in the world—especially of those—whoever they may be—with whom I happen to be in company. . . . No one can think more highly of the understanding of women than I do. In my opinion, nature has given them so much that they never find it necessary to use more than half.' (Oxford ed., pp. 113-14.)

There was, in fact, in Bath at or about this period a young clergyman 'of about four or five and twenty'—he was, to be precise, twenty-six years old—who answered very well in personal appearance to the description of Henry Tilney; he was 'rather tall, had a pleasing countenance, a very intelligent and lively eye, and, if not quite handsome, was very near it'—the Reverend Sydney Smith. Sydney Smith, moreover, like Henry Tilney, was remarkable for the 'fluency and spirit' of his talk and had a notable vein of 'archness and pleasantry in his manner', to which innumerable contemporaries bore witness. 'He was an admirable joker,' said Brougham, 'he had the art of placing ordinary things in an infinitely ludicrous point of view'; Frances Kemble wrote of 'the fanciful fund and inexhaustible humorous drollery of his conversation among his intimates'; Francis Horner of his 'mixture of odd paradox, quaint fun, manly sense, striking language'. Many more such tributes could be quoted,[1] but one has only to look at his letters and the surviving specimens of his talk to see that Sydney Smith's shrewd, lively banter, by turns ironical and extravagant, was of very much the same brand as Mr. Tilney's. The specimens of Mr. Tilney's conversation quoted above would all, I think, pass muster in Sydney Smith's *Life and Letters* without any suspicion of alien origin—indeed, they would be accepted as characteristic. Jane Austen had reproduced, on the lips

[1] See Hesketh Pearson, *The Smith of Smiths*, Hamish Hamilton, 1934, pp. 15-20.

of Mr. Tilney, the very note of drollery that so captivated the hearers
of Sydney Smith. Was this really a fortuitous coincidence?

Sydney Smith's situation at this period is described in the collection of his letters edited by Mr. Nowell Smith and recently published
by the Clarendon Press. After two or three years spent as curate at
Netheravon (some thirty miles from Bath) under the patronage of
Mr. Michael Hicks Beach, M.P., with whose family he had developed
a cordial friendship, he was about to take up his duties in Edinburgh
(whither he set off in May 1798) as tutor to his patron's son. 'In the
meantime,' says Mr. Nowell Smith, 'we know that he stayed at Bath,
where his father was living, and in London and at Williamstrip, and
that he had busied himself in finding a governess for the Hicks
Beach daughters.'[1] He found a suitable governess in Bath in the
spring of 1797, and it is from Bath that we find him writing to Mr.
Hicks Beach some six months later, dating his letter from Edgar
Buildings, on 19 January 1798. His letter is occupied largely with his
patron's family concerns: the daughters were evidently in Bath under
the charge of their newly-found governess:

'I have seen your little Girls [he says], they are looking extremely
well. I called upon their fair preceptress this morning without finding
her at home; she has relaxed from the rigor of her System, and we
are to see them all to dinner on Friday. There is a Letter laying at
Williamstrip or Netheravon for me, which I will thank you to forward. I am sorry to hear that Michael and William have both the
whooping cough. I am in daily expectation that Michael [his prospec-
tive pupil] will write me word, that himself, and his brother are
better. The Dykes have dined with us; my Father likes them very
much, and is quite astonished that the clods have stuck to their
Shoes so little. They say that there are 10,000 strangers now in Bath.
. . . Will you remember me very kindly to my good friend Mrs. Beach
and tell her I hope she will employ me if she has any commissions at
Bath. I shall be very anxious to hear something about this whooping
cough.'

He concludes with kind remembrances from his 'father and family'.
His next letter, undated, is written to Mrs. Hicks Beach from

---

[1] *The Letters of Sydney Smith*, ed. Nowell C. Smith, Clarendon Press,
1953, p. 7.

3 Edgar Buildings; she has evidently sent him her commission and he has busied himself in executing it:

'The lightest of the 2 Stuffs is 8d, and the other 7d pr yd, $\frac{1}{2}$ yd wide; the yellow, and blue, and white striped linsey 15 Nails wide, at 14d; the other pattern is a serge $\frac{7}{8}$ wide, at 22d if bought in small, and 21 in large quantities—no deductions for the others. The yd wide stuff at 11d turned ought to be good for nothing. If you should determine to lay in a stock of these stuffs, I will send you any quantity you chuse; do not be under any anxiety about transmitting me the money.—I shall see you in the Summer and am quite rich enough to wait till then. You will not scruple I am sure to tell me, if I have executed your commission imperfectly, and to employ me in any way that I can be of farther use to you. I walked 26 Miles and then got into a Coach which overtook me. My Father and Mother are extremely happy in the idea of seeing Mr. B and you at Ba, and beg to be kindly remembered—I hope Mr. B. will vote against our perfidious administration. Mrs. Fowle's name is not in the Pump room books, perhaps you can obtain her address from Mr. Fowle of Dur.[1]

Does it involve too wide a stretch of the imagination to suppose that the young clergyman who sought materials for Mrs. Hicks Beach at Bath in January 1798, was the same as the young clergyman who discussed materials in the Lower Rooms so learnedly with Mrs. Allen and her niece, and that he had actually been encountered by the creator of these characters when she herself was visiting the Rooms a week or two before? Readers of Jane Austen will remember

[1] Mr. Nowell Smith (p. 14) says that 'Dur' is 'no doubt an abbreviation of a place-name'; I suggest Durrington, some two and a half miles from Netheravon. He queries 'turned' in the sentence beginning 'The yd wide stuff'; I would rather question whether 'ought' (in 'turned ought') should not be 'out'. Of the Fowles, Mr. Nowell Smith observes that they were 'neighbours of the Hicks Beachs at Netheravon'; I do not know whether any more precise identification can be made. In Jane Austen's letters of this period there are frequent references to the family of the Rev. Thomas Fowle (1727–1806), Vicar of Kintbury, Berks, and Rector of Allington, Wilts; her sister Cassandra was engaged to one of his sons; for full particulars see Index II in Dr. Chapman's *Jane Austen's Letters*. Allington is seven or eight miles from Netheravon.

how Mr. Tilney came to the rescue when Mrs. Allen was concerned about a possible tear in her sleeve:

' "I am afraid it has torn a hole already; I shall be quite sorry if it has, for this is a favourite gown, though it cost but nine shillings a yard."

' "That is exactly what I should have guessed it, madam," said Mr. Tilney, looking at the muslin.

' "Do you understand muslins, sir?"

' "Particularly well; I always buy my own cravats, and am allowed to be an excellent judge; and my sister has often trusted me in the choice of a gown. I bought one for her the other day, and it was pronounced to be a prodigious bargain by every lady who saw it. I gave but five shillings a yard for it, and a true Indian muslin."

'Mrs. Allen was quite struck by his genius. "Men commonly take so little notice of those things," said she: "I can never get Mr. Allen to know one of my gowns from another. You must be a great comfort to your sister, sir."

' "I hope I am, madam."

' "And pray, sir, what do you think of Miss Morland's gown?"

' "It is very pretty, madam," said he, gravely examining it; "but I do not think it will wash well; I am afraid it will fray." '

It is tempting to infer that some such conversation as this passed between Jane Austen (or some one of her party) and the Reverend Sydney Smith in the Rooms at Bath in November or December 1797, and was recollected by her when she drew her picture of the Reverend Henry Tilney in the early months of 1798. There is no *a priori* improbability in such a meeting; rather the reverse, for Jane Austen must have been well acquainted with the Hicks Beaches: 'I am sorry,' she wrote to Cassandra, on 9 January 1796, 'for the Beaches' loss of their little girl, especially as it is the one so much like me';[1] she moved (see her Letters *passim*) among families—Chutes,

---

[1] *Letters*, ed. Chapman, p. 4. It must be to the loss of this daughter that Sydney Smith alludes when he writes to Mrs. Hicks Beach on 11 January 1796 (*Letters*, ed. Nowell Smith, p. 7): 'Pray remember me very kindly to Mr. B. I feel for you both sincerely, may God make those children which remain dutiful and amiable.' This proves the correctness of Sydney Smith's dating of his letter, upon which some doubt is cast in Mr. Nowell Smith's note.

Withers, and Bramstons—with whom the Hicks Beaches were connected;[1] and there seems, as we have observed, to have been a particular link among the Fowles. Jane Austen and Sydney Smith, in the little world composed of the '10,000 Strangers' then in Bath, must have belonged to social circles which were almost if not quite coincident. Moreover, their respective lodgings in the Paragon and Edgar Buildings were (as Professor Garrod has pointed out to me) only a minute's walk apart.

I myself find the inference of such a meeting almost irresistible, in spite of a possible objection to it. The authors of the *Life and Letters*, as we have seen, imply (they do not give any supporting evidence) that the Austens left Bath immediately before Christmas 1797. Sydney Smith's letter, written from Edgar Buildings and asking for commissions from Mrs. Hicks Beach, is dated 19 January 1798. While there is no decisive evidence as to the date of his arrival in Bath—it *might* have been before the Austens left for Christmas—the tone of this letter suggests that it was but recent. The references to the whooping cough, and 'the Dykes have dined with us', compel, it is true, the conclusion that the writer had been in Bath at least some days; but the news of the Misses Hicks Beach ('I have seen your little girls'), and the request for commissions from Mrs. Hicks Beach, suggest that this is the first letter he addressed to the Hicks Beach household after his arrival; and that he had arrived but recently may perhaps be inferred from a sentence quoted above from his letter to Mrs. Hicks Beach: 'I walked 26 Miles and then got into a Coach which overtook me'.

A *terminus post quem* for the beginning of his visit is provided by two letters written by him from Bowood in December 1797;[2] in the first, he tells Mr. Hicks Beach that as soon as he has celebrated the impending marriage of his brother, he will 'return to Oxford from hence and then set off immediately for Netheravon'; in the second letter, written to Mrs. Hicks Beach on Friday, 8 December, he confirms this intention: 'from hence [Bowood] I shall make the best of my way to Oxford, pack up my things, and get to Hungerford at

[1] See *A Cotswold Family* by Mrs. William Hicks Beach, Heinemann, 1909, pp. 256–7.
[2] *Letters*, ed. Nowell Smith, pp. 11–12.

about 2 o'Clock on Tuesday next, where I should be very much obliged to you if you would send a horse for me.' He can hardly have been in Bath, therefore, before the middle of December. If he did go to Bath then, he might have met the Austens there between say, the 15th and the 22nd. Even if he did not reach Bath till the following month, after the Austens had left it, it does not follow that we must abandon the identification: he may have been staying with his parents in Edgar Buildings in November, before he was called to Bowood,[1] or there may have been a meeting between him and Jane Austen in the Rooms on some earlier, unspecified, occasion when they were in Bath together.

For an epilogue we may turn to J. E. Austen Leigh's *Memoir* of his aunt, where, writing in 1870, he quotes from the recollections of his brother-in-law, Sir Denis Le Marchant: 'I have heard Sydney Smith, more than once, dwell with eloquence on the merits of Miss Austen's novels. He told me he should have enjoyed giving her the pleasure of reading her praises in the "Edinburgh Review".' True, there is no word of his ever having met her; but, if the supposed meeting did take place, there was no reason why, on the publication of *Northanger Abbey*, he should have recognized himself in Mr. Tilney, or have associated the creator of that character with the young lady with whom he had made a fleeting—and probably forgotten—contact in the Assembly Rooms more than twenty years before.

[1] 'They have sent for me here' he says, writing from Bowood on December 1, and that might mean that they had summoned him from Bath. In the same letter, it is true, he speaks of *returning* to Oxford; but he was still a Fellow of New College, no doubt with rooms there, and he might well speak of 'returning' there even if it was from Bath that he had come to Bowood.

In Memoriam[1]

O n 15 September 1833 Arthur Hallam died in Vienna. He
was only twenty-two; he had achieved nothing in the
world; he left behind him a handful of undistinguished
poems and a few pages of prose; and yet by the charm
of his conversation and the force of his personality, by all that did
not survive his death, he impressed beyond measure those who
knew him; his was the most remarkable genius that Mr. Gladstone
had ever encountered; and his contemporaries at Eton and Cambridge
were agreed that in him England lost one who would have been
ranked among her greatest men.

On 1 October the news of his death reached Tennyson. The friends
had known each other for five years; both had belonged to the
'Apostolic' set at Cambridge; and they were drawn closer together by
Hallam's engagement to Tennyson's sister Emily, which took place
in 1831. When both friends had left the University and Hallam himself was in practice at the Bar, this link bound him to the Tennyson
family, and caused him often to make the difficult journey to their
home at Somersby:

> *How often, hither wandering down,*
> *My Arthur found your shadows fair,*
> *And shook to all the liberal air*
> *The dust and din and steam of town:*
>
> *He brought an eye for all he saw;*
> *He mixt in all our simple sports;*
> *They pleased him, fresh from brawling courts*
> *And dusty purlieus of the law. . . .*

[1] Introduction to the Nonesuch Press edition of *In Memoriam*, 1933.

In Memoriam

O bliss, when all in circle drawn
About him, heart and ear were fed
To hear him, as he lay and read
The Tuscan poets on the lawn.

In the intervals between such visits they corresponded. It is a pity that Tennyson's letters to Hallam should have been destroyed; but Hallam's letters to him and to his sister show clearly enough the terms of their friendship both at the University and during the few remaining years of his life: many common interests, in literature, in politics, in philosophy, in art; a common circle of friends; a worship on the part of Tennyson the full depth of which seems never to have been suspected by its object, nor, indeed, perhaps by Tennyson himself during the lifetime of his friend. It was a friendship, above all, of the mind.[1]

The two would travel together abroad, in Devon, Cornwall, Yorkshire; they would 'talk over literary plans for the future'; they 'interchanged thoughts on the political state of the world . . . had grave arguments about the Church. The unsettled condition of the country and the misery of the poorer classes weighed upon them'. Both were handsome, both were eager, both were earnest, though Hallam's earnestness was as genial as his friend's was sombre. Tennyson would send his verses, and receive in exchange criticism and reflections on the wider topics that interested them both. Throughout Hallam writes in a rallying, and sometimes in a casual

[1] It may be left to others to make the most of such references as 'hands so often clasped in mine', or Tennyson's strange dream on the eve of being offered the Laureateship. Another glimpse of his 'subconscious' may be of interest to the psychologist: in 1846 he visited Switzerland, keeping a journal in the MS book in which he wrote *The Princess*; it was during this tour that he wrote the song that ends with the celebrated line 'And murmuring of innumerable bees'. On 10 August he noted in the MS book, 'Summit, crowd of people, very feeble sunset, tea, infernal chatter as of innumerable apes'. If anything is needed to clinch the resemblance of these last half-dozen words to the concluding line of 'Come down, O maid', is it not the fact that *apes* is the Latin word for 'bees'? [It appears—see J.H. Buckley, *Tennyson The Growth of a Poet*, Harvard, 1960 —that Tennyson wrote 'innumerous', which his son, in his *Memoir*, transcribed as 'innumerable'; so perhaps it was Hallam's 'sub-conscious', and not his father's that was responsible for the echo.]

[98]

tone; a tone which makes the reader feel that 'dear old Alfred' was valued higher than Hallam's other intimate friends chiefly because he was a great poet—'the greatest', Hallam prophesied, 'of the century'—and because he was the brother of Emily. 'Fare thee well, old trump,' he writes in 1832, 'poems are good things but flesh and blood is better. I only crave a few words'; and in July 1833 he writes to Tennyson in Scotland: 'I feel to-night what I own has been too uncommon with me of late, a strong desire to write to you. I do own I feel the want of you at some times more than at others; a sort of yearning for dear old Alfred comes upon me; and that without any apparent reason. . . . However I hope you are not unpleasantly employed in the land of cakes and broiled fish.'

To Tennyson, on the other hand, his friend was, quite simply, in his own words, 'as near perfection as mortal man could be'. The news that came in October 1833 was to affect him to the depths, not for a few years, but for the remainder of his life.

How deeply he was affected is shown best not by *In Memoriam*, which was written in the years immediately succeeding Hallam's death, and in order to express the grief that it inspired, but by poems which were not written primarily to express his sorrow, when Hallam's death was a thing of the very distant past. Thirty years later, visiting a stream by which they had walked together, he still could write:

> All along the valley, while I walk'd to-day,
> The two and thirty years were a mist that rolls away;
> For all along the valley, down thy rocky bed,
> Thy living voice to me was as the voice of the dead,
> And all along the valley, by rock and cave and tree,
> The voice of the dead was a living voice to me.

There is a still more remarkable testimony to the depth of his grief. When, an old man of eighty, Tennyson published *Demeter*, the volume contained a poem which shows that even the passage of more than fifty years had not changed his heart. It is the somewhat nebulous piece entitled *Vastness*, in which the poet considers the infinity of time and the infinity of space, and contrasts with them the littleness of man and man's concerns:

In Memoriam

Raving politics, never at rest—as this poor earth's pale history
*   runs,—*
What is it all but a trouble of ants in the gleam of a million
*   million suns?*
What is it all, if we all of us end but in being our own corpse-
*   coffins at last,*
Swallow'd in Vastness, lost in Silence, drown'd in the depths of a
*   meaningless Past?*
What but a murmur of gnats in the gloom, or a moment's anger of
*   bees in their hive?*

Peace, let it be! for I loved him, and love him for ever: the dead
*   are not dead but alive.*

After half a century there is no doubt to what centre his roving mind,
however wide its wanderings, will return.

Even later, in his last volume of all, Tennyson bears witness in *The
Silent Voices* to the presence that still haunts his dreams:

When the dumb Hour, clothed in black,
Brings the dreams about my bed,
Call me not so often back,
Silent Voices of the dead. . . .

In Memoriam, which has been not absurdly described as 'perhaps
the richest oblation ever offered by the affection of friendship at the
tomb of the departed', was a monument to this unassuageable
affliction.

In Memoriam did not appear till 1850—seventeen years after the
death that it commemorates. It was very different from any poem
that had ever then been written. Looking at it now, when Tennyson
is an old-fashioned writer and *In Memoriam* a classic, we may forget
that the poem designed in the years that followed 1833 was in
several ways unprecedented. On the one hand no English poet had
attempted so long and so elaborate an elegy; on the other hand no
poet had put into an elegy such overwhelming passion. By the side of
In Memoriam Gray's *Elegy* seems impersonal, *Lycidas* frigid, even
Adonais distant, the lament of a poet for a poet, not of one friend for

another. Even the most touching of previous elegists had not struck so personal a note, except on the rarest occasions—as when Cowley writes on Hervey, or Dryden on Oldham—and none had sustained it; other writers invite us, for a moment, to share their grief; to offer to share Tennyson's lonely and enduring sorrow would be impertinent.

It is not easy, today, to appreciate the poem's extraordinary qualities: it is known too well, and it is usually read in fragments. It may well seem thus a series of lyrics not very remarkable for anything except felicity of expression. One of its earliest critics said that *In Memoriam* would never lose its appeal because it expresses just those feelings which will through all ages affect ordinary men and women. It is true that it does express such feelings; but to say that and no more gives a very misleading idea of the quality of the poem as a whole. Reading one or two of its hundred 'sections' the ordinary man may appropriate them to himself and to his own grief, but he will do so at the cost of forgetting how extraordinary was the passion of which the whole poem is the record, and how extraordinary an achievement it was to record that passion in a single elegy written on so huge a scale.

In Memoriam is unlike any other elegiac poem in the way in which it combines depth of feeling with elaboration of design. For it is an exceedingly artificial composition. The outpourings of grief are drilled and marshalled into a quite arbitrary formation. In a sense, though not a word of it is not sincere, the whole poem is an elaborate fraud. Various analyses of *In Memoriam* have been attempted; all agree that the poem, with its well-spaced references to the passage of the seasons and to the recurrent days of anniversary, is meant to appear to be a record of the first three years after Hallam's death. A little inquiry shows that this appearance is quite illusory: in the words of A. C. Bradley, 'We know that certain sections were written soon after Arthur Hallam's death. We have good grounds for believing that certain others belong to 1836–7. One or two we can date about 1840 and we have some rather doubtful evidence that not a few others fall between that year and the publication of the poem.' Their ostensible order is deliberately misleading. When the poem appeared, the manifestation of such a carefully cultivated grief gave some offence. It was thought to be morbid: 'much shallow art', it was said, had been 'wasted on tenderness shown to an Amaryllis of the Chancery Bar'; seventeen years had elapsed since Amaryllis' death; it was time that his admirer turned to something else. Even one of his most sympathetic critics, writing years later, wondered how Tennyson could have included in *In Memoriam* the stanzas beginning:

> *Oh sorrow wilt thou live with me*
> *No casual mistress but a wife.*

Those who made these criticisms were at least aware of the difference between *In Memoriam* and the poems which express the first passionate outburst of the mourner's anguish, and it is true that to see Tennyson in the immediate agony of his grief we must turn to *Break, Break, Break*, to *The Two Voices*, and perhaps to the undated 'Epilogue' appended to his son's *Memoir*:

> *Speak to me from the stormy sky!*
> *The wind is loud in holt and hill,*
> *It is not kind to be so still:*
> *Speak to me, dearest, lest I die.*

> *Speak to me, let me hear or see!*
> *Alas, my life is frail and weak:*
> *Seest thou my faults and wilt not speak?*
> *They are not want of love for thee.*

These verses are as moving as anything in *In Memoriam* itself, but they do not belong to it, and it was a right instinct that caused their author to exclude them. That single naked cry in the midst of his elaborate symphony would have exposed, not indeed any insincerity in the rest of the poem, but the artificiality of its context.

There is another feature of *In Memoriam* the originality of which is easily forgotten: the attempt, unlike any that had been made before, to interweave with its personal theme a philosophy 'adequate to the needs of the day', or as Professor Sidgwick put it, 'the *forward* movement of the thought'. The poem is a record, not merely of grief, but of a struggle between two things in the poet's mind.

In Memoriam

Tennyson was not a philosopher, and his utterances on religious and metaphysical questions bear all the marks of a mind that has devoted to those topics much reflection but little thought. In his letters, in his recorded conversations, even in his poems, there is a wealth of platitude expressed in philosophical language: such language when innocent of philosophic thought is always sickening in its effect: the cant of the unthinking idealist is fully as unpleasant as that of the unthinking materialist. Such topics as those discussed in *Vastness* continually occupied Tennyson's meditations. His was a mind of the type that is impressed by the supposed philosophical importance of geological and astronomical discoveries. He was intensely aware of the conflict, then beginning, between faith and scientific knowledge, but he never understood the essential conditions of such a conflict. On the one hand, his was not a religious mind—of poetry that can be called mystical he has not left a single line—he could not put by one side of the controversy with the serenity of faith, and wonder at scientific discovery simply as a revelation of the detail in the physical world. On the other hand, his heart forbade him to think that religious feeling was of a kind with our other feelings, and that all those were merely states of body: men could not, he felt (and feeling for him decided such matters) be mere 'magnetic mockeries', condemned to rot in their 'own corpse-coffins'. When such a conclusion was suggested, then, in his own words:

> *A warmth within the breast would melt*
> *The freezing reason's colder part,*
> *And like a man in wrath the heart*
> *Stood up and answer'd 'I have felt'.*

Placed in this dilemma, his lack of real intellectual power betrayed him; he was unable to think things out, and he never achieved that impartiality which comes from a philosophical view of the 'conflict': it never occurred to him that there could be no clash because the opponents were not fighting on common ground. He shared the illusion common to the orthodox and their opponents—that 'Science' was incompatible with Christianity, that the descent of our species from another helped to prove that there was no God—without

[103]

enjoying either the comfort of unquestioning faith or the security of complete scepticism. He was sensitive and he was conscientious, and he suffered. The traces of that suffering, and his attempts to come to terms with it, may be seen throughout *In Memoriam*.

There are places in *In Memoriam* where the inadequacy of the thought reveals itself so clearly that it interferes with our enjoyment of the poem:

> *Not only cunning casts in clay:*
> *Let Science prove we are, and then*
> *What matters Science unto men,*
> *At least to me? I would not stay.*

> *Let him, the wiser man who springs*
> *Hereafter, up from childhood shape*
> *His action like the greater ape,*
> *But I was born to other things.*

That is poor philosophy and poor poetry. Tennyson does not express something transcending reason; he reduces the tone of the passage to the level of argument (he even uses italics to bring home his point), and then he refuses to think. Tennyson's reflective poetry is often marred by such defects; in *In Memoriam* there are fewer than there might be, because there grief for the most part stifles even the desire to think, and he is content to feel without arguing.

In Memoriam thus reveals the mainspring of Tennyson's philosophy and his religion: he was not strong enough to despair. Again and again in the poem he says it, almost in so many words: ' a love as deep as mine cannot, in the nature of things, be for a perishable object; a creature so fair and noble as my dead friend cannot be doomed to annihilation'. And the force of the 'cannot' is simply this: 'I cannot believe that it is so'; and the impossibility of believing it is grounded not really in the nature of things but in Tennyson's own nature: he 'could not' believe it, for if he had believed it he could not have lived. Indeed in the last months of 1833 his grief did drive him to play with thoughts of suicide, as *The Two Voices* very clearly shows, and his only escape was a half-philosophy, founded on feeling instead of thought. At the end of his life he summed it up in a line already quoted:

Peace, let it be! for I loved him, and love him for ever: the dead
are not dead but alive.

Here he states quite simply the transition from feeling to belief, and leaves the reader to infer that the one is grounded on the other. It is where he feels that he must find arguments to prove that consequence, that the poetry is spoiled; in *In Memoriam*, fortunately, he is usually content to let grief alternate with a hope which he cannot explain:

And I—my harp would prelude woe—
I cannot all command the strings;
The glory of the sum of things
Will flash along the chords and go.

Fully to appreciate *In Memoriam* we must bear in mind something of what has just been said about the conditions in which it was composed. But it is not, after all, in its philosophy, or in the record of its author's experience, that lies its chief appeal. They alone could never save it from oblivion. It is read today, or at least it is worth reading, simply for the poetry that it contains. Tennyson was perhaps the most accomplished poet who has ever written in English, and *In Memoriam* contains much of his finest work; indeed, it would be strange if it did not; he was writing in the fullness of his powers under the influence of the deepest emotion that he had ever felt. And that emotion was all-pervading. It is this comprehensiveness that saves the poem from becoming tedious, and gives us, instead of a monotonous dirge, a collection of lyrics varying widely in their content—expressing different states of mind and feeling, describing now external nature, now the poet's own imaginative visions. Tennyson's grief quickened his senses, and served also to draw all his experiences on to a single thread. 'I mingle all the world with thee,' he declared, and this omnipresence of Hallam's image, while it made him feel everything around him more acutely, made everything a fitting subject for the verse in which he expressed his grief:

In Memoriam

Thy voice is on the rolling air ;
I hear thee where the waters run ;
Thou standest in the rising sun,
And in the setting thou art fair.

So too each season spoke the same message in its special voice—
and in no poem are the peculiar qualities of the seasons conveyed
more subtly:

But Summer on the steaming floods,
And Spring that swells the narrow brooks,
And Autumn, with a noise of rooks,
That gather in the waning woods,

And every pulse of wind or wave
Recalls, in change of light or gloom,
My old affection of the tomb,
And my prime passion in the grave.

By an art which evades analysis, he makes landscapes live, and conveys not merely a picture of their visible features, but the atmosphere
that fills them, endowing them, as a painter too can endow his
landscapes, with the observer's own emotion. They recall the couplet
of an earlier poet, in whose work the same gift is at times displayed:

All these were sad in nature, or they took
Sadness from him, the likeness of his look.

These are the highest moments of *In Memoriam*, when an exquisite
description of nature conveys unerringly a deep emotion:

Calm is the morn without a sound,
Calm as to suit a calmer grief,
And only, thro' the faded leaf
The chestnut pattering to the ground.

Calm and deep peace on this high wold,
And on these dews that drench the furze,
And all the silvery gossamers
That twinkle into green and gold. . . .

In Memoriam

Calm and deep peace in this wide air,
 These leaves that redden to the fall;
 And in my heart, if calm at all,
If any calm, a calm despair:

Calm on the seas, and silver sleep,
 And waves that sway themselves in rest,
 And dead calm in that noble breast
Which heaves but with the heaving deep.

Again (one can do no more than quote):

Now fades the last long streak of snow,
 Now burgeons every maze of quick
 About the flowering squares, and thick
By ashen roots the violets blow. . . .

Now dance the lights on lawn and lea
 The flocks are whiter down the vale,
 And milkier every milky sail
On winding stream or distant sea;

Where now the seamew pipes, or dives
 In yonder greening gleam, and fly
 The happy birds, that change their sky
To build and brood; that live their lives

From land to land; and in my breast
 Spring wakens too; and my regret
 Becomes an April violet,
And buds and blossoms like the rest.

In the consecutive sections which begin 'I climb the hill' and 'Unwatch'd, the garden bough shall sway' (C, CI) he achieves the same effect, and again with even greater art in the pieces (XV, LXXII, XCIX, CVII, for instance) describing the cloud and sun, the wind and calm, which go to make up what we call a 'day': this, for instance, is a description of the anniversary of Hallam's death:

[107]

In Memoriam

Lift as thou may'st thy burthen'd brows
  Thro' clouds that drench the morning star,
  And whirl the ungarner'd sheaf afar,
And sow the sky with flying boughs,

And up thy vault with roaring sound
  Climb thy thick noon, disastrous day;
  Touch thy dull goal of joyless gray,
And hide thy shame beneath the ground.

It is by these pieces that *In Memoriam* best deserves to live; these, and the sections, fewer in number, where Tennyson turns inward his minute and subtle power of observation and gives us directly, and not in the mirror of external nature, a record of his emotion, and yet resists the temptation to philosophize or preach upon it:

Be near me when my light is low,
  When the blood creeps, and the nerves prick
  And tingle; and the heart is sick
And all the wheels of Being slow.

Be near me when the sensuous frame
  Is rack'd with pangs that conquer trust;
  And Time, a maniac scattering dust,
And Life, a Fury slinging flame.

Or the lines where he describes how he spent a summer night in the fields, reading the letters of his friend:

So word by word, and line by line,
  The dead man touch'd me from the past,
  And all at once it seem'd at last
The living soul was flash'd on mine,

And mine in this was wound, and whirl'd
  About empyreal heights of thought,
  And came on that which is, and caught
The deep pulsations of the world,

In Memoriam

Aeonian music measuring out
The steps of Time—the shocks of Chance—
The blows of Death. . . .

The 'trance' ceases with the coming of dawn, described in lines which, in their kind, have never been surpassed by any poet:

Till now the doubtful dusk reveal'd
The knolls once more where, couch'd at ease,
The white kine glimmer'd, and the trees
Laid their dark arms about the field:

And suck'd from out the distant gloom
A breeze began to tremble o'er
The large leaves of the sycamore,
And fluctuate all the still perfume,

And gathering freshlier overhead,
Rock'd the full-foliaged elms, and swung
The heavy-folded rose, and flung
The lilies to and fro, and said

'The dawn, the dawn,' and died away;
And East and West, without a breath,
Mixt their dim lights, like life and death,
To broaden into boundless day.

For such passages as these, *In Memoriam* will continue to be read, even by those who are most conscious of its faults—of its inadequate philosophy, its occasional lapses of taste (most noticeable when Tennyson tries to poeticize domestic incidents), and its affected diction.

Yet there are readers who will never like *In Memoriam*, and that for the very good reason that they do not like Tennyson himself. Tennyson was a very individual artist, and *In Memoriam* is the most Tennysonian of all his poems. To lovers of Tennyson it makes therefore a particularly strong appeal; to others it may well seem irritating

and monotonous. The metre imposed on him very definite limitations, and though within its bounds he achieved a marvellous freedom by varying his pauses and his periods, as the poem goes on we
become familiar with these devices, and can to a certain degree
forecast which, out of a limited number of possible modulations, he
will use. Still his dexterity has surprises always in store—no one
could have anticipated, for instance, the suspension of the last word
in the following stanza:

> *Abiding with me till I sail*
> *To seek thee on the mystic deeps,*
> *And this electric force, that keeps*
> *A thousand pulses dancing, fail.*

Repetition is a device which he uses continually, and in a dozen
different ways, often achieving his effects without making it plain
how they are obtained. Sometimes each stanza (as in the pieces
'Calm is the morn' and 'Be near me', quoted above), sometimes each
line, begins with the same, or with a cognate, word:

> *And all we met was fair and good,*
> *And all was good that Time could bring,*
> *And all the secret of the Spring*
> *Moved in the chambers of the blood—*

and the following form is typical:

> *A distant dearness in the hill,*
> *A secret sweetness in the stream. . . .*

Sometimes he repeats, only once, a single word, as in the line 'The
breaker breaking on the beach', where the repetition seems to give a
sense of the futility of the recurrent movement it describes.

Sometimes the repetition is not exactly verbal, as in a stanza—
almost a self-parody—occurring in one of the three pieces never published with the rest of the poem (though originally written for it)
and first printed by Hallam Tennyson in 1897:

> *Another whispers sick with loss:*
> *'O let the simple slab remain!*
> *'The "Mercy Jesu" in the rain!*
> *'The "Miserere" in the moss!'*

All these are typical of a formula which occurs, with variations, so often in *In Memoriam* that those who let it get on their nerves must find it difficult to appreciate the poem.

Perhaps Tennyson's favourite device in *In Memoriam* is that of ending a section by elaborating or expanding an idea which in its context carries little or no emotional or other weight. In XXXVI the poet devotes three stanzas to describing how the Incarnation came about and the Gospels were written; in the fourth and last stanza, which is a quarter of the poem, all that he has to say may be summed up in the words 'which he who runs may read'; he chooses to say it thus:

> *Which he may read that binds the sheaf,*
> *Or builds the house, or digs the grave,*
> *And those wild eyes that watch the wave*
> *In roarings round the coral reef.*

Here there is an expansion within an expansion, for the last couplet means nothing more than 'savages'. Yet it is curiously right and effective that the piece should end thus, and it is difficult if not impossible to say why. Again, CXVII is a poem of three stanzas; in it Tennyson declares that time is working on his side; by keeping him from Hallam it is increasing the joy that will be felt when in the end they meet; delight at their reunion will, he says, 'a hundred fold accrue'

> *For every grain of sand that runs,*
> *And every span of shade that steals,*
> *And every kiss of toothed wheels,*
> *And all the courses of the suns.*

There is an unaccountable but irresistible felicity in this disproportionate elaboration of the idea of Time.

There will always be some who like and some who hate poetry which shows as obviously as does Tennyson's the labour of the file. Writing a poem of some thousand stanzas, all in the same strict metre, he was almost forced to be a *virtuoso*. To save his poem from monotony, he had to use every technical device at his command; shifting the accent, lengthening and shortening the clauses of verse, varying the pauses, changing the *tempo*. Those who read the poem with ordinary care will see that with reference to *In Memoriam* these are not set, unmeaning phrases, but describe the methods which Tennyson very consciously and carefully employed to make the beauty of his verse. Seventeen years went to its composition, and for the rest of his life he was continually altering its *minutiae*, changing a word here and there, occasionally a line, more usually an apostrophe or a stop. He found nothing of any substance that he wished to alter. The poem of his youth, into which he put himself completely as an artist and as a man, stood, with all its idiosyncrasy of feeling and expression, as a work by which he was ready to be judged.

Oscar Wilde after Fifty Years[1]

Passion, prejudice and hypocrisy have converged upon the name of Oscar Wilde and combined to obscure and to distort the story of his downfall. Not a few of those who were involved in the tragedy were alive until the other day, so that tenderness towards personal susceptibilities, besides regard for conventional decorum, has restrained several witnesses who might have given a first-hand account of many aspects of the case: and those who have acknowledged no such restraints have not always been those most likely to be scrupulous or accurate in their testimony. Each of the two leading figures has, it is true, left us his version (or versions) of the affair; but the most illuminating passages of Wilde's *apologia* (which make up more than half the complete version of *De Profundis*) were, until very recently, inaccessible; while Lord Alfred Douglas's self-vindications are so frequently marred by hysteria and delusion, and contradict each other so often and so wildly, that no reliance can be placed upon his uncorroborated word. Of the independent witnesses perhaps the most knowledgeable and the least reticent was Frank Harris; but he, unfortunately, seems never to have cared, or even to have known, whether or not what he was telling was the truth. As for the writing of Wilde's life, too often those who have undertaken it have been either sentimental apologists or merely 'popular' biographers.

It is Wilde himself who has suffered most from the resulting obscurity: *omne ignotum pro horrifico*: the veil that decency has drawn over the particulars of his story has left full scope to Mrs. Grundy and Tartuffe, who have vied with each other in heaping execration on his name. And even those who have clung to the quite untenable

[1] 1951.

opinion that Wilde was wrongly convicted, or have pleaded that his was what is glibly excused as a 'pathological case', have for the most part accepted the view that he was the evil genius, not only of many casual acquaintances, but even of his closest friend.

After half a century, it is possible to attempt a comprehensive examination of the evidence and a dispassionate judgment of the characters involved. The tragedy was essentially a tragedy of character, but it is only upon a basis of ascertained fact that a true estimate of the characters can be formed. Such an estimate must, it seems, take into account the following conclusions.

First, the verdict against Wilde was legally correct, and the acts of which he was accused must be accepted, on his own admissions, as instances of conduct that had become habitual with him during the years immediately preceding his conviction. Nor is there any ground for complaint concerning the conduct of the trials (save the stupid attempt to use against the prisoner what he—and others—had written as an author—an attempt which recoiled upon the heads of those who made it); indeed, the fact that Wilde came so miraculously near to escape was due to the fairness of the procedure and the efforts of Sir Edward Clarke (to whom at the time Douglas professed his 'profoundest gratitude and admiration', but whom he afterwards attempted to traduce). The verdict was inevitable; whether the sentence was appropriate is, of course, a matter of opinion.

Further, none of the persons with whom Wilde was proved to have had guilty relations can be said to have been in any sense 'corrupted' by him; their own conduct and antecedents make this plain enough. Douglas himself had compromised himself with a blackmailer before he met Wilde, and it seems that he consistently pursued a course in matters of sex parallel with and independent of that followed by his friend. As for his relations with Wilde himself, he admitted in his *Autobiography* that they were not entirely innocent, as he had hitherto invariably asserted them to be; but this was evidently a brief phase in their relationship, and deeply emotional though their friendship was, the element of sex very soon passed out of it. Douglas's admission, however, is proof (if further proof be needed) of the hypocrisy with which, in *Oscar Wilde and Myself*, he pretended that it was not until after the trial that he began to suspect the possibility of Wilde's guilt: 'low, coarse, abominable brute' is a fair specimen of the epithets which in that scurrilous production he heaped upon his friend for indulging in practices to which he himself was equally addicted.

Above all, the new *De Profundis* must kill for ever what Wilde himself called the 'infant Samuel theory', the theory that postulated the 'influence of an elder over a younger man'. 'Outside of a small set in those two cities [London and Oxford],' wrote Wilde, 'the world looks on you as the good man who was very nearly tempted into wrong-doing by the wicked and immoral artist, but was rescued just in time by his kind and loving father.' That theory still holds the popular field. But it will not survive a reading of the evidence now available, in the light of which the accepted roles must be virtually reversed. *The Green Carnation*—shrewd and brilliant though it is— tells but half the truth, and its picture of the innocent Lord Reggie Hastings, dancing to the tune piped by the somewhat sinister Mr. Amarinth, is altogether misleading. The relationship of Rimbaud with Verlaine affords a truer parallel. In each case it was the younger man that was the dominant party—and dominant to a really terrifying degree. Douglas, no doubt, was fascinated by Wilde's gifts and flattered by his patronage; but Wilde, for his part, was—there is no other word for it—enslaved. The story of the friendship is a pitiful tale of time and money, talent and reputation, and in the end almost life itself, thrown away on a charming but utterly selfish and inferior being.

In the passages of *De Profundis* now first published, Wilde recalls to his friend's mind the hard facts of the matter.

'When I tell you that between the autumn of 1892 and the date of my imprisonment I spent with you and on you more than £5,000 in actual money, irrespective of the bills I incurred, you will have some idea of the sort of life on which you insisted. Do you think I exagger- ¿ te? My ordinary expenses with you for any ordinary day in London —for luncheon, dinner, supper, amusements, hansoms and the rest of it—ranged from £12 to £20, and the week's expenses were naturally in proportion and ranged from £80 to £130. . . . And though it may seem strange to you that one in the terrible position in

[115]

which I am situated should find a difference between one disgrace and another, still I frankly admit that the folly of throwing away all this money on you, and letting you squander my fortune to your own hurt as well as to mine, gives to me and in my eyes a note of common profligacy to my bankruptcy and makes me doubly ashamed of it.'

But, of course, the expenditure of money was of small, or only of symbolic, importance.

'Most of all I blame myself for the entire ethical degradation I allowed you to bring on me. The basis of character is will power, and my will power became absolutely subject to yours. It sounds a grotesque thing to say, but it is none the less true. Those incessant scenes that seemed to be almost physically necessary to you and in which your mind and body grew distorted and you became a thing as terrible to look at as to listen to: that dreadful mania you inherit from your father, the mania for writing revolting and loathsome letters: your entire lack of any control over your emotions, as displayed in your long resentful moods of sullen silence, no less than in your sudden fits of almost epileptic rage . . . these, I say, were the origin and causes of my fatal yielding to you in your daily increasing demands. You wore me out. It was the triumph of the smaller over the bigger nature. It was the case of that tyranny of the weak over the strong which somewhere in one of my plays I describe as being "the only tyranny that lasts".'

Wilde made really desperate efforts to free himself from that tyranny; time and again, at his insistence, the relationship was actually severed. Time and again his efforts were thwarted; sometimes by Douglas himself (who would cross half Europe and send ten-page telegrams threatening suicide if his friend did not take him back); sometimes by what seems a fatality (the tragic death of Douglas's brother caused Wilde to relent at a crucial moment); always with the aid of a deep vein of tenderness in Wilde himself on which Douglas knew well how to play. The record of it all is set down by Wilde, who sums up without irony a situation that was indeed ironical: 'but for my pity and affection for you and yours, I would not now be weeping in this terrible place'.

Finally, it must be accepted that Douglas was responsible for Wilde's imprisonment in a manner even more direct; it was his insensate desire to see his father in the dock that caused Wilde to institute the fatal prosecution.

'To see him "in the dock", as you used to say: that was your one idea. The phrase became one of the *scies* of your daily conversation. One heard it at every meal. Well, you had your desire gratified. . . . For two days you sat on a high seat with the Sheriffs, and feasted your eyes with the spectacle of your father standing in the dock of the Central Criminal Court. And on the third day I took his place.'

Even at that late stage the final act in the tragedy might have been averted; had it not been for Douglas's insistence that he should stay, that his flight would have been a 'score' for Queensberry, Wilde might have yielded, either before or after his first prosecution, to friends who entreated him to flee the country—though an invincible belief in his lucky star, a determination to 'face the music', and a refusal to betray those to whom pledges were due, would probably have kept him in England in any event.

But Douglas's responsibility goes farther still. There is even ground for saying that, in respect of certain specific charges at his trial, connected with incidents at the Savoy Hotel, Wilde refrained from challenging evidence which, seen in its proper light, would have implicated his friend and not himself. He was optimistic, no doubt, when he suggested that by challenging that evidence he could have secured his own acquittal on all the charges; but one cannot doubt his sincerity when he says: 'I have never regretted my decision for a single moment, even in the most bitter moments of my imprisonment. . . . To have secured my acquittal by such means would have been a life-long torture to me. But do you really think you were worthy of the love I was showing you then, or that for a single moment I thought you were?'

De Profundis, of course, gives Wilde's own, *ex parte*, account of the matter. But devastating though the indictment is, at all essential points the story it contains rings true. The voice which tells it, though the tones are passionate, is none the less measured and deadly; Wilde speaks almost without bitterness and quite without hysteria.

'I have now written, and at great length, to you [he concludes] in order that you should realize what you were to me before my imprisonment, during those three years' fatal friendship; what you have been to me during my imprisonment, already within two moons of its completion almost; and what I hope to be to myself and to others when my imprisonment is over. I cannot reconstruct my letter or rewrite it. You must take it as it stands, blotted in many places with tears, in some with the signs of passion or pain, and make it out as best you can, blots, corrections, and all. As for the corrections and errata, I have made them in order that my words shall be an absolute expression of my thoughts. . . . As it stands, at any rate, my letter has its definite meaning behind every phrase. There is in it nothing of rhetoric. . . . I will admit that it is a severe letter. I have not spared you. Indeed you may say that, after admitting that to weigh you against the smallest of my sorrows, the meanest of my losses, would be really unfair to you, I have actually done so, and made scruple by scruple the most careful assay of your nature. That is true. But you must remember that you put yourself in the scales.'

The justice of the judgment thus passed by Wilde upon his friend is abundantly confirmed above all by Douglas's own reaction to it: he did not answer *De Profundis*, he destroyed it. Perhaps he supposed that he had destroyed the case against himself. He did not know that Wilde's faithful friend Ross had preserved the text which would one day put the world in possession of the truth.

That, of course, is not Douglas's version of the matter. When, years afterwards, in his (unsuccessful) libel action against Mr. Arthur Ransome, he was confronted with the full text of *De Profundis* (copied from the manuscript which Ross had presented to the British Museum), he asserted that the letter was completely new to him: Ross, he said, had failed to deliver either the original or a copy of the text, in accordance with the instructions which Wilde gave on his release. In that assertion Douglas persisted to the end.

Here is a plain, irreconcilable contradiction on a fundamental issue. On which side the truth lies it is hardly possible to doubt: Douglas, many times over a self-confessed perjurer, is accusing Ross, Wilde's faithful friend, of a gross betrayal of his trust—and (loyalty apart) of a purposeless betrayal, for if on Wilde's release his first concern (as Douglas himself asserted) was to keep the two friends apart, why should he have suppressed this violent attack of the one upon the other? Nothing, one would suppose, could have suited his purpose better.

Once having taken up this attitude, however, Douglas could not abandon it. Thereafter, any mention of *De Profundis* induced in him an insensate fury which vitiates his comments on it even in 'A Summing-Up', where he speaks of 'the Puritan cant, smug falsity and sloppy sentiment (to say nothing about a regular cascade of split infinitives) of *De Profundis*'. The sneer does little credit to its author and is indeed out of keeping with the prevailing tone of his retrospect, which is chastened and moderate. The mood of 'all passion spent' pervades the book; the hereditary devil of hatred which inspired *Oscar Wilde and Myself* has been exorcised (perhaps by the Catholic Church?) and there emerges a human being, vain and unreasonable, but not wholly uncharitable or unattractive. Lord Alfred deals skilfully with the embarrassing apologia of Mr. Sherard (who in his *Life* attempted to excuse Wilde's criminal acts by suggesting that they were committed during quasi-epileptic states which were followed by complete amnesia), and with the naïve (or was it cynical?) invitation of Bernard Shaw to present Wilde's story as a comedy and not a tragedy. Compared with any of his previous effusions about his own past, this is a generous and honourable survey, and one is glad that it is its author's last word upon the matter.

In one respect, indeed, Lord Alfred's 'Summing-Up' serves as a corrective to Wilde's *Epistola*: Wilde certainly exaggerated the sterilizing effect of the friendship upon his own creative gift. To say 'during the whole time we were together I never wrote one single line' is (exactly what Wilde denies that he is doing) to use the language of rhetorical exaggeration. On the other hand, Douglas claims a larger share of the credit for *The Ballad of Reading Gaol* than he is entitled to: contemporary letters make it plain that the poem was almost finished before Wilde left Berneval to rejoin his friend in Naples. The truth is, no doubt, that 'Bosie' played a double role for Wilde the artist as he did for Wilde the man: he stimulated and disorganized his powers, just as he inspired and ruined his life.

'People must adopt some attitude towards me and so pass judgment both on themselves and me.' The judgment that the law and society pass upon the crime of which Wilde was guilty has not altered, and is not likely to be altered substantially—not, at least, so long as 'enlightenment' in this matter consists in regarding those who share Wilde's tendencies not as criminals but as lunatics or lepers—cases, as the smug phrase has it, for the doctor rather than the policeman. And though Wilde came out of prison a different and in many ways a chastened being, it was not of his crime that he repented.

'I don't regret for a single moment having lived for pleasure . . . [he wrote]. I don't feel at all ashamed of having known them [the "evil things of life"]; what I do feel ashamed of is the horrible Philistine atmosphere into which I was brought. . . . What is loathsome to me is the memory of interminable visits paid by me to the solicitor Humphreys, when in the ghastly glare of a bleak room I would sit with a serious face telling serious lies to a bald man till I really groaned and yawned with ennui. There is where I found myself, right in the centre of Philistia, away from everything that was beautiful or brilliant or wonderful or daring. I had come forward as the champion of respectability in conduct, of Puritanism in life, and of morality in art. *Voilà où mènent les mauvais chemins.*'

'The one disgraceful, unpardonable, and to all time contemptible action of my life was to allow myself to appeal to Society for help and protection.' The Society to which he appealed passed its judgment upon Wilde for what he did. But the final judgment upon him, as upon everyone else, must be based not on what he did but on what he was.

On what he was: to the moral qualities of Wilde friend and enemy have alike borne witness: his enemies by their silence, his friends by their devotion. The malice that was directed against him after his downfall was intense: 'Wilde will never lift his head again,' said a shrewd observer, hearing of his conviction, 'for he has against him all men of infamous life.' But not even the most hostile of his critics ever denied him the virtues of gentleness and courage, gaiety and magnanimity, or attributed to him a mean action or an unkind word. His freedom from bitterness throughout his sufferings is quite beyond praise, and almost beyond belief.

Oscar Wilde after Fifty Years

The quality of the friendships he inspired, the devotion shown by those who stood by him in adversity and to the end, notably Reginald Turner and Robert Ross, speaks still more strongly in his favour.

'When I was brought down from my prison to the Court of Bankruptcy, between two policemen, Robbie waited in the long dreary corridor that, before the whole crowd, whom an action so sweet and simple hushed into silence, he might gravely raise his hat to me, as, handcuffed and with bowed head, I passed him by. Men have gone to heaven for smaller things than that. I have never said one single word to him about what he did. I do not know to the present moment whether he is aware that I was even conscious of his action. It is not a thing for which one can render formal thanks in formal words. I store it in the treasure house of my heart. I keep it there as a secret debt that I am glad to think I can never possibly repay. . . .'

The man who inspired that action, and thus acknowledged it, was not lacking in nobility.

It is, of course, in *De Profundis* itself that the most intimate picture of Wilde's character is to be found: *Mon coeur mis à nu* might indeed have served as a sub-title for the book. It is always difficult to fix the *vraie vérité* about a personality at once complex, artificial and introspective. And where an attempt at self-portraiture is made by a person so prone to dramatization as was Wilde, so given to a 'literary' handling of his material, and (one must add) with so inviting a subject for dramatic treatment, a reader may be forgiven for wondering whether the result shows the writer as he was, or as he saw himself—or merely as he wished to appear to others. Many readers of the original *De Profundis* have felt that the panegyrics of suffering and simplicity, and the lyrical passages about the 'fascination' and the 'charm' of Christ, which make up so large a part of the book, have about them something maudlin if not actually insincere; that the penitent in white raiment was but a new pose of the inveterate *poseur*; and that by his repeated protestations that 'the supreme vice is shallowness' he succeeded only in showing how deep his own shallowness went.

The full *Epistola* should correct, by an altered perspective, any such impressions. The 'purple' passages take their place in an impassioned argument which is itself closely interwoven with the personal narrative that now forms the larger part of the book. That narrative explains how Wilde came to learn 'the hate of hate, the scorn of scorn, the love of love' which he proclaims as his new gospel, and attests the sincerity with which he proclaims it. Douglas and Douglas's father had taught him not only where they are led who allow their lives to be ruled by hate—that was their tragedy—but where they find themselves who live according to no rule at all—and that was his. If in reflecting on these bitter discoveries he falls into the error of excess and fine writing, those who remember the conditions in which his letter was composed will forgive him the literary fault.

Prison was not the last act in Wilde's drama. Not many weeks after he had been released and the text of *De Profundis* placed in Lord Alfred's hands, the two resumed their life together. One might have supposed that a meeting between the author and the victim of that denunciation was possible on one footing only: that Douglas must have undergone the change of heart for which Wilde had pleaded and come forward to help him in the task of rebuilding his shattered life; how otherwise, one may ask, could the two have faced each other? But it was not so. There is no record of that meeting; one can only conclude that nothing was forgotten and all forgiven. The two natures had become complementary and could not keep apart: 'Everyone is furious with me for going back to you, but they don't understand us. I feel that it is only with you that I can do anything at all.' Again Wilde was the sufferer, but this time the uneasy union did not last long: 'When you are not on your pedestal you are not interesting'; and Douglas soon left Wilde to the care of friends whose affection for him was made of a finer and more durable material.

In that epilogue, which lasted from his release in April 1897, until his death on 30 November 1900, lay the real and final tragedy of Wilde's life. Douglas slurs it over discreetly in a few pages of his 'Summing-Up'; its stages can be traced in the scattered letters to his friends, from Berneval, from Naples, from Switzerland, from Rome, from Paris, which have been collected in the volumes *After Reading* and *After Berneval* and elsewhere. Gradually his faith in the possibility of any future for himself diminishes; his powers decay;

'having lost position, I find my personality of no avail'; his distractions—of which the most innocent were the camera and the bicycle—lose their charm; the entire hold on life is loosened. The depressing scene is lit by gleams of the old wit and the old fantasy—now, alas! too often employed to wheedle money from his friends—and one sees why those friends found him, even when he was impossible to defend, impossible not to forgive.

Wilde, of all men, according to Bernard Shaw, has the strongest reason to tell posterity to read his works and to forget his life. Shaw stated, with his usual exactness, the opposite of the truth. Apart from one perfect play, one memorable poem and the new, full version of *De Profundis*, Wilde left little with which, as literature, posterity need seriously concern itself. He was a brilliant writer of letters and teller of stories, and a master of the epigram and the aphorism; but his successes in these genres belong not so much to his work, into which he put his talent, as to his life, for which (as he said) he reserved his genius. The story of that life—not yet adequately treated by a biographer—will never lose its poignant appeal to those whose study is human nature or human society. Never was a drama so crude, so terrible in its *dénouement*, acted in a setting so brilliant, so luxurious, so well designed to enhance its tragic element. For the light it throws on the principal actor in that tragedy—himself a permanent type of the artist whose life was his material—his *Epistola: in Carcere et Vinculis* must always remain a living work.

A Shropshire Lad at Fifty[1]

A Shropshire Lad is as old today as *In Memoriam* was in 1900. The moment is a suitable one for a review of Housman's standing as a poet, and a glance at the controversies that his verse seems destined perpetually to provoke. Was Housman, even at his most successful, truly a poet—or was he merely a writer of accomplished verses? What, after all, is poetry? Wherein is the secret of the effectiveness that distinguishes it from verse? What should be, and what in this case was, the relation of poetry to the poet's experience?

During the present century a great range of possibilities has been opened to the writer for the first time. Verse and prose have been made the vehicles not merely of rational discourse, not merely of articulate emotion, but of picture, idea, image, so disposed as to reproduce the phantasmagoria of the writer's own sub-consciousness or to evoke emotion in the reader by touching directly, or with the least possible mediation of the intellect, springs which lie below the level of the conscious mind. Mr. T. S. Eliot and James Joyce have been among the pioneers, in prose and verse, of writing of this kind in England. There is still dispute whether some writers have not pushed unprofitably far their experiments along these lines, but there is no denying that they have opened up new and fruitful fields for literature, and revealed much that was hitherto imperfectly understood about the effectiveness of writings in more familiar kinds.

The main issues in the current phase of this perennial debate were strikingly summed up by Housman himself in the lecture on 'The Name and Nature of Poetry' which he delivered before the University of Cambridge in 1933. Poetry, he says in effect, usually (though

[1] 1946.

[124]

it need not always do so) takes the form of verse; its main function is to communicate, or at least to arouse, emotion, and its effectiveness varies ordinarily with the quality and depth of the thoughts and sentiments that it conveys. But not only in accordance with these: there is an element in poetry, and it is the essentially poetic element, that consists not of thinking and sentiment, but of ideas and images, and works through their purely suggestive power. If that element is lacking, no utterance, however sublime, however deep, however moving, really deserves the name of poetry.

Many lines and stanzas, and even whole lyrics, which are among the most moving in our poetry (and the same is true, though less often, of snatches of prose) appeal to us solely by virtue of the second of these elements—the mysterious effectiveness of words and images which act not merely as sounds, but still less as elements in a complex of thought, which makes no appeal to the intellect except that it should recognize the meaning of words and grasp the structure of simple sentences, and which possess no emotional significance other than that somehow inherent in certain ideas as symbols or sources of suggestion.

The best examples of such poetry in English are the lyrics of Blake, though the Symbolist school in France and their English disciples have exploited more fully the possibilities of *la poésie pure*. In Blake we find poetry, in Housman's words, 'disengaged from its usual concomitants, from certain things with which it naturally unites itself and seems to blend indistinguishably', from nobility of sentiment, for instance, and depth of thought. 'Blake again and again, as Shakespeare now and then, gives us poetry neat, or adulterated with so little meaning that nothing except poetic emotion is perceived and matters':

> *A fathomless and boundless deep,*
> *There we wander, there we weep;*
> *On the hungry craving wind*
> *My Spectre follows thee behind.*

'I am not equal,' Housman declared, 'to framing definite ideas which could . . . correspond to the strong tremor of unreasonable excitement which [such] words set up in some region deeper than the mind.'

Hence follows the conclusion that poetry is 'more physical than intellectual', which Housman sought to confirm by a striking account of his reactions to others' poetry and of his method of composing his own. The 'symptoms'—the bristling of the skin, the 'precipitation of water to the eyes', the shiver down the spine—will be familiar to readers of poetry; the method of composition—'there would flow into my mind, with sudden and unaccountable emotion, sometimes a line or two of verse, sometimes a whole stanza at once, accompanied, not preceded, by a vague notion of the poem which they were destined to form part of'—though unusual, particularly in a poet whose work is so intellectually precise as Housman's, is, of course, by no means without parallel.

Some words of warning should be added to what Housman and others have written on this subject. Recognition of the non-intellectual element of poetry and of the physical effect of poetry upon a sensitive organism must not mislead us into attributing undue importance to that element, or exalting the physical test into a criterion of what is poetry and what is not. Even lyrical poetry—and, far more, poetry of the dramatic, tragic and reflective kinds—may demand the co-operation of the reader's mind for its appreciation. As for the physical criterion, it is no test of the 'purity' of poetry— for a complex and reflective poem may equally bring tears to the eyes; nor even of aesthetic quality—for tears may be evoked even in the most fastidious of judges by cheap melodrama or oratory, by the strains of military music, or by a sentimental situation in the theatre or in real life. The physical criterion is so obviously subjective (being at the mercy of circumstance, of mood, and the idiosyncrasies of the individual reader) that it cannot be appealed to in any field as a sovereign touchstone. Further, familiarity blunts this particular edge, and a poem is liable to lose this special magic, while retaining its other effective qualities, when one knows it well.

How far, then, did Housman respond to the influences—evidently well understood by him—that were at work in the field of poetry during the half-century before his death? And to what extent did he himself contribute to them? The answer to both these questions is, unambiguously, not at all. Thoroughly conventional in form, in diction, in substance, the verse he published in 1922 was the same as the verse of *A Shropshire Lad*, and there was no difference, in these respects, in any of his posthumously published poems. Though now and again a young admirer paid him the tribute of imitation, he cannot truthfully be said to have exercised any influence on the poetry of his day. As a poet he lived in a vacuum, shut off from the developments of his time; one need only consider Gerard Manley Hopkins and Mr. Eliot to appreciate, by contrast, the completeness of his isolation.

The tests suggested by Housman in his lecture may, however, without difficulty and not without profit be applied to his own poetry. The strong appeal that it makes to his admirers is not derived from its intellectual or its moral content. Housman is not a philosophical or an imaginative poet: he displays no Wordsworthian insight into the deep springs of human sympathy, no Shakespearian understanding of the range and intensity of human passions. Nor is his an example of the 'pure' poetry with which his lecture was so much concerned and towards which so much of contemporary poetry seems to be aspiring: it is not difficult to understand, but it must be understood if it is to be felt. Housman's poems are likely to suffer more than most from the application of the physical tests which he himself described; with a few notable exceptions they are devoid of that element of strangeness which is an almost necessary constituent of the poetry that sends the shiver down the spine. Moreover, they gain their effects rather by the description or expression of recognizable emotions than by reliance on the suggestive properties of image or idea: his sentiments are precise, not only in the centre (so to say) but round the edges; his arrows are stiff and do not quiver in the wound.

> *Ay, look: high heaven and earth ail from the prime foundation;*
> *All thoughts to rive the heart are here, and all are vain:*
> *Horror and scorn and hate and fear and indignation—*
> *Oh why did I awake? When shall I sleep again?*

A Shropshire Lad *at Fifty*

Housman's method is well exemplified in that third line: even when he feels most deeply, he tries to tell us exactly what it is he feels.

That Housman is a 'pure' poet, therefore will scarcely be suggested. Whether he is a 'classical' or a 'romantic' poet, whether he is a 'great' poet, whether he is properly speaking a poet at all—these are questions which have been hotly and fruitlessly debated.

A Cambridge mathematician once observed that too many philosophical controversies could be reduced to the following form: A: *I went for a walk to Trumpington this afternoon.* B: *I deny it: I did nothing of the sort.* So, many of the arguments about Housman's claim to the title of a poet, and about the merits of his work, when they are not quarrels about the definition of terms, are really nothing but statements of the predilections of the participants, cast in disputatious form. Housman's work is particularly liable to provoke such disputations because he inspires very strong feelings, of admiration and the reverse, and the best service that the critic can perform is to attempt not to assess his claim to literary ranks and titles but to throw some light on the qualities of his poems and to suggest what it is in them that provokes such diversity of opinion.

Housman spoke of the 'narrow measure' of his verses, and the epithet is just in more senses than one. He published in his lifetime only a hundred or so short lyrics; about seventy more were brought out by his brother after his death. Almost all are concerned with a few familiar themes: passionate affection for the living—

> *Ah, past the plunge of plummet,*
> *In seas I cannot sound,*
> *My heart and soul and senses,*
> *World without end, are drowned.*

> *His folly has not fellow*
> *Beneath the blue of day*
> *That gives to man or woman*
> *His heart and soul away—*

[128]

A Shropshire Lad *at Fifty*

desiderium for the dead—

> *The night is freezing fast,*
> *To-morrow comes December;*
> *And winterfalls of old*
> *Are with me from the past;*
> *And chiefly I remember*
> *How Dick would hate the cold—*

the brevity of human life, and the vanity of human wishes. *Immortalia ne speres* is his recurrent message, and a contemptuous but dignified acquiescence in the 'foreign laws of God and man' is his counsel to the reader who resembles him in being

> *a stranger and afraid*
> *In a world I never made.*

Such comfort as he finds has two sources: pride in the maintenance of an unfaltering attitude in the face of destiny and pleasure in the beauties of nature as displayed in the countryside he knew. In life, no doubt, he had other resources, chief among which was the pursuit of classical learning; but this was a distraction rather than a comfort. While it may have helped him to forget his inner unhappiness, it cannot actually have diminished it; and his 'interests' find no place in his poetry.

Almost every poem bears the impress of his personal idiom in diction and versification, not least the score or so in which, speaking in the character of a country boy, sometimes in his native county and sometimes exiled in London among crowds of 'men whose thoughts are not as mine', he describes romantic situations which involve not infrequently death in battle or at the hangman's hands. Such poems have attained celebrity and praise out of proportion to their number and their merit: some of those in which this convention plays the largest part are among his few unquestionable failures:

> *When I came last to Ludlow*
> *Amidst the moonlight pale,*
> *Two friends kept step beside me,*
> *Two honest lads and hale.*

I

A Shropshire Lad *at Fifty*

Now Dick lies long in the churchyard,
And Ned lies long in jail,
And I come home to Ludlow
Amidst the moonlight pale.

There is Housman at his most easily recognizable and at his worst—
the familiar ingredients displayed almost with the effect of self-
parody. But in many of his finest poems he draws upon this stock-
in-trade hardly at all—whether he is inspired by his consciousness of
human destiny:

When I meet the morning beam
Or lay me down at night to dream,
I hear my bones within me say
'Another night, another day. . . .'

or by personal affection:

If truth in hearts that perish
Could move the powers on high,
I think the love I bear you
Should make you not to die. . . .

This long and sure-set liking,
This boundless will to please,
—Oh, you should live for ever
If there were help in these. . . .

or by external nature:

And like the cloudy shadows
Across the country blown
We two fare on for ever,
But not we two alone.

With the great gale we journey
That breathes from gardens thinned,
Borne in the drift of blossoms
Whose petals throng the wind;

[130]

A Shropshire Lad *at Fifty*

Buoyed on the heaven-heard whisper
Of dancing leaflets whirled
From all the woods that autumn
Bereaves in all the world.

These examples are all drawn from *A Shropshire Lad*, but equally moving poems are to be found throughout his work, and in a large majority of them the 'bucolic convention' plays no part whatever.

Those who do not care for Housman's poetry, however, will hardly like his successes better than his failures: the finish, the accomplishment, the clearness of the cut, that delight his admirers, and the charm that makes them uncritical in their admiration—these will only increase the distaste of those to whom Housman's voice is distasteful; for that voice is audible in every line, and there is nothing so repellent as the charm that fails in its enchantment, particularly if it is as insistent as is Housman's. And I, says Tennyson,

> *And I—my harp would prelude woe—*
> *I cannot all command the strings;*
> *The glory of the sum of things*
> *Will flash along the chords and go.*

There are no such wild reliefs for Housman or his readers—no flashes or gleams from another world; he commands perfectly his strings and himself, and himself is all he has to offer.

This intransigence limits his effectiveness. Housman, like Gray (and no doubt for a like reason) 'never spoke out'; heartfelt as his lyrics are, they are never *cris de coeur*; among the children of unhappiness his kinship is with Heine, not with Emily Brontë. Poetry did not free his spirit; it was a key for the locking, and not for the unlocking, of his heart.

In his own words, his poems were to him what the pearl is to the oyster—a morbid secretion. Such models, such sources of inspiration as he had were indeed (we have his word for it) of the most 'romantic' kind—the Bible and the old ballads; and the feelings which forced him to write were deep and painful and 'romantic' too; but they were defined and cut into 'polygons with hard edges' before they became matter for his verse—at what deep levels, often below consciousness, we know from the account of his method of composition already quoted.

A good deal has been written, by those to whom Housman's poetry is uncongenial, about his 'pose of pessimism', his 'faked emotions', his 'sham pastoral convention'. That Housman's verse lacked spontaneity—or, rather, often lacked the appearance of it—is undeniable; many of his poems, indeed, are clearly the fruit of a process (never, one suspects, deliberate, and often quite unconscious) of self-dramatization. But to discount this habit of self-dramatization as a 'pose' betrays a misunderstanding of Housman's personality, which, though it might have been defensible fifty years ago, has no excuse since the publication of his posthumous poems. Several of these make very plain the nature of the emotions which were evidently his strongest source of inspiration, and among them their editor, Mr. Laurence Housman, draws particular attention to the following:

> *Ask me no more, for fear I should reply;*
> *Others have held their tongues, and so can I;*
> *Hundreds have died, and told no tale before;*
> *Ask me no more, for fear I should reply . . .*

The 'reply' is found in the succeeding stanza, and most clearly in the indignant outburst beginning

> *Oh who is that young sinner with the handcuffs on his wrists?*

of which his brother declares that 'it says something which A.E.H. very much wished to say, but perhaps preferred not to say in his own lifetime'.

'Friendship,' says Housman's biographer, 'had once meant for him a whole-hearted devotion which its objects were not always able to repay in kind,' and which, one may add, it was not easy for a reticent man to express in poems meant for publication:

> *Because I liked you better*
> *Than suits a man to say,*
> *It irked you, and I promised*
> *To throw the thought away.*

A Shropshire Lad *at Fifty*

Herein lies the reason for Housman's use of a bucolic convention and his persistent dramatization of himself. The convention enabled him to express emotions which he shrank from exposing undisguised; the imaginary or the internal drama was the expedient by which a frustrated nature sought unconsciously to compensate itself for the lack of those emotional contacts—the life and adventure of the heart—for which the lyric impulse craves, so that it may have the matter that it needs if it is to fulfil itself.

The distinction between 'sincerity' and 'artificiality' is not appropriate to such a case. It is enough to say that those who re-read *A Shropshire Lad* in the light of *The Name and Nature of Poetry* and of its author's own posthumously published verses will learn an interesting lesson about the varieties of poetic inspiration and poetic method.

Housman Obscured[1]

nyone who has read Housman's poems with an eye to the experience that lay behind them must have perceived that those of them which express personal affection are poems not of normal love but of passionate friendship. The fact had not escaped the notice of his biographers. 'It is plain,' wrote Mr. A. S. F. Gow, twenty years ago, 'that friendship had once meant for him a whole-hearted devotion which its objects were not always able to repay in kind.' Some of his posthumous poems, threw a still clearer light upon the unhappiness of the man and the inspiration of the poet:

> *He would not stay for me : and who can wonder?*
> *He would not stay for me to stand and gaze.*
> *I shook his hand and tore my heart in sunder*
> *And went with half my life about my ways.*

For any who wished to trace these emotions nearer to their source, unmistakable signposts were displayed in the lines prefixed to Housman's edition of Manilius and inscribed 'SODALI MEO M. I. IACKSON' and in the reminiscences of his brother Laurence, who records (among other things) that A. E. H. spoke of that same friend of Oxford days as 'the man who had more influence on my life than anybody else'. Jackson was an athlete and something of a Philistine; he shared lodgings in London with Housman after they had both gone down from St. John's, married early, and spent most of his life abroad. Housman's devotion to him was life-long, and 'Mo's last letter' was found by Laurence carefully preserved among his brother's papers after his death. These facts have long been public

[1] A review of *A. E. Housman : A Divided Life*, by George L. Watson, 1958.

[134]

property. Read the poems with them in mind and the story they tell will be clear—or clear enough.

There a biographer might well be content to leave the matter. Does one want, ought one to want, to pry further, to spy into the private, personal, relationship? This is a question that has arisen often in connexion with the Lives of the Poets, and it may be that 'students of literature' are more inclined nowadays to answer it in the affirmative than they used to be. Perhaps one does want to drag the skeleton of dead love from the cupboard, and perhaps there is nothing wrong in doing so: the artist who has put his life into his work can hardly complain of the critic who seeks to spell out of that work the life that lies concealed in it. 'With this key Shakespeare unlocked his heart'—a literary historian may claim the right, may even feel that it is his duty, to put an eye to the keyhole.

In *A. E. Housman: A Divided Life*, Mr. G. L. Watson has applied his eye to the keyhole of the sported oak at St. John's, and of the doors where Housman's 'heart was used to beat' at 82 Talbot Road, W.11, and Byron Cottage, Highgate, and other abodes of his youth—but alas! it is dark inside and all he can see is two half-lit figures and a little of the furniture. His publishers tell us that he has made a 'challenging reappraisal' and achieved 'the first comprehensive interpretation' of Housman's 'enigmatic figure'; but in truth little of his newly discovered material is significant, and he has nothing really 'revealing' to reveal. His investigations have brought to light a handful of facts about Housman's ancestry, his home-life, his school-days, and his early manhood, and a couple of interesting photographs of Moses Jackson; but when he embarks on the story of the poet's inner experience and his emotional relations with his friend he has to depend upon such evidence as is supplied by the poems themselves and upon his own imagination.

To interpret evidence, and to control imagination where evidence fails, a biographer needs knowledge, sympathy and judgment. Mr. Watson's deficiencies in these respects have led him, in his attempt to 'probe the origins' and lay bare the 'obscure psychological sources' of Housman's poetry, to produce a portrait which, though sympathetic in intention, is sadly lacking in delicacy and in truth.

Mr. Watson evidently feels pity and even affection for the man he supposes Housman to have been. But affection is one thing, sympathy another. To paint a truly sympathetic portrait of a man it is not necessary to like him—affection, indeed, may falsify the picture—but it is necessary to understand him, and you cannot understand a man unless you know him and the world he lived in. To Mr. Watson, England in the reign of Victoria (and in particular the Oxford and Cambridge which formed the background and the foreground of Housman's life) is as distant, as shadowy, as unreal as ancient Rome to a schoolboy. As soon as he takes his eye from the keyhole and attempts to paint a picture he is lost; he becomes a victim of the cliché and the catchword. He thinks about the past in terms drawn from the programme of an historical pageant: for him, yeomen are sturdy, the eighteenth century is 'placid', the Edwardian Age 'bland', the twentieth century 'hectic'.

A Wardour Street conception of history does not matter so much when the author is writing about Housman's remote ancestors, but when we reach the reign of Victoria it falsifies the picture of the world in which his life was lived. It is here that Mr. Watson's habit of writing and thinking, in clichés most fatally betrays him: he is obsessed with the catchword 'Victorian'; we meet it on every other page: 'Victorian efficiency', 'Victorian authority', 'Victorian etiquette', 'Victorian religion', 'adamant Victorian code', 'sterling Victorian principles', 'the frostbound climate of Victorian morality'. An all-round boy who lived in the reign of Queen Victoria becomes 'the Victorian equivalent of an all-round boy'—as if *real* all-round boys did not then exist. As for young men: 'the charming and benign aspects of nature provided not only the daily environment of most young men, but a solvent to their intellectual perplexities'.

This inability to see things (and people) except through 'literary' spectacles vitiates Mr. Watson's treatment of his central theme—the emotional relationship which was the most important factor in Housman's development both as a poet and as a man.

We must suppose ourselves in Oxford in the autumn of 1878: 'In the wake [says Mr. Watson] of the Oxford Movement and the period of Blue China, the intellectual currents flowed as gently as the Cherwell . . . while in the streets and courtyards, on that early October day, the neophytes loitered in awkward and awestruck expectancy.'

Among the 'neophytes' was young Moses Jackson; and the relationship between Jackson and Housman is the main theme of Mr. Watson's book. It is a subject that needs insight and delicacy of treatment—the development of a romantic devotion that was to last as long as Housman's life. How did it begin? No doubt, as Mr. Watson says, the answer is simple: 'two people had met . . . and liked each other'—*parceque c'était lui, parceque c'était moi*. But unfortunately he is not content to leave the matter there. He points out that Housman chose Propertius as a special book for Mods., and the choice, he tells us, was 'decisive':

'For Propertius was not simply a Latin author whose garbled works invited extensive editorial revision, but a poet of the most powerful and passionate order. Contagiously emotional and erotic, his verse could hardly fail to stir the blood of any young scholar; and Housman's scholarship, it has been generally agreed, was of a kind that excelled in sensitive perception. . . . The secret writhings of sexuality were laid bare as he read Propertius, while in the presence of Jackson's vigorous and magnetic youth the cold intimations of death began to dissolve. . . . Anything but pagan in his habits or disposition, Jackson brought to life, nevertheless, a figment of that remote Roman world whose passions throbbed in the *Elegies* of Propertius.'

To one who sees his subject through spectacles of books, it seems as simple as that: Housman was a 'sensitive' scholar, Propertius an 'erotic' poet; Housman was tasting what Mr. Watson calls 'the drowsy syrup of Jackson's friendship' just at the time when he was exposed, in working hours, to the 'inflammatory material' of Propertius's *Elegies*; small wonder that before long 'Jackson had literally become' (as Mr. Watson puts it) 'Housman's consuming interest.'

If Mr. Watson suspected the real meaning of 'sensitive' as applied to a scholar, if he knew a little about Propertius, if he knew anything about undergraduates, could he suppose that Housman's liking for Jackson turned to passion under the influence of the *Elegies* of Propertius?

[137]

Housman Obscured

Why did Housman fail in Greats? That is the next problem that faces Mr. Watson. It is hard to explain why so well equipped a classical scholar should have collapsed so completely, and why the failure should have produced in him, at any rate for a time, so shattering an effect.

The problem has baffled all those who have written about Housman. Mr. Gow was content to record that he chose 'rather to spend his time over the text of Propertius than to devote himself to the pursuits proper to a Greats candidate'—suggesting that it may have been fastidiousness that prevented him from showing up answers to many of the questions set. That is a plausible explanation as far as it goes; but (like Housman—might one say?—in the examination) it leaves a number of questions unanswered.

Mr. Watson connects Housman's failure directly with the central emotional experience of his life. In this he may be right; but, if so, the precise nature of the connexion, exactly what it was that happened, must remain uncertain. Mr. Watson thinks that he can tell us: shortly before Greats, he says, Housman discovered 'to his shame and horror' the depth of his feeling for his friend. That such a discovery should have first been made after three years of close companionship seems strange enough; still more improbable is the reaction suggested:

'To Housman the very existence of such impulses could only be regarded as a hideous revelation. . . . From the moment when he began to suspect the nature of his attachment to Jackson, Housman would have been overcome by the sense of a disaster for which he was criminally at fault, while the long jovial evenings turned into nightmares of duplicity, and the once pleasurable days stretched into a nerve-wracking interminable tight-rope. . . . His failure in Greats was, after this, the next step and minor consequence.'

'Shame and horror . . . hideous revelation . . . criminally at fault'—all this (to Mr. Watson the inevitable 'Victorian' reaction) is pure conjecture—and it is not consistent with what Housman has disclosed of his feelings on the subject. He did not doubt that such a love must lead to frustration: 'Eternal fate so deep has cast Its sure foundation of despair'—but that he did not think it 'shameful' or 'hideous' he has left clear testimony, not only in his bitter satirical verses about 'the colour of his hair' but, as plainly, in *Last Poems*:

> *The laws of God, the laws of man,*
> *He may keep that will and can;*
> *Not I: let God and man decree*
> *Laws for themselves and not for me. . . .*

'Their deeds,' he says, 'I much condemn.' To impute to Housman shame and horror at such a discovery is to misunderstand him, and the misunderstanding is vital, for it is Mr. Watson's thesis that this discovery and his reaction to it fixed once and for all the whole course and character of Housman's life and poetry.

What is the evidence connecting this discovery (supposing it to have taken place) with Housman's failure in Greats? Here we have an example of the rashness with which Mr. Watson forces Housman's poems into the service of the biographer. In this instance the evidence—he calls it 'solid evidence'—consists of the poem 'Parta Quies', which Housman contributed in 1881 to an undergraduate magazine called *Waifs and Strays*:

> *Goodnight; ensured release,*
> *Imperishable peace,*
>   *Have these for yours,*
> *While sea abides and land,*
> *And earth's foundations stand,*
>   *And heaven endures.*
> *When earth's foundations flee,*
> *Nor sky nor land nor sea*
>   *At all is found,*
> *Content you, let them burn:*
> *It is not your concern;*
>   *Sleep on, sleep sound.*

'In the light of this exquisite threnody, spilling from the heart of a young man of twenty-two,' asks Mr. Watson, 'what *had* Housman been doing? What could precipitate, in the midst of enjoyable studies and sympathetic friends, so dark a lament?' One wonders why this little poem—'exquisite' perhaps, but hardly 'dark'—should provoke this question, until one realizes that Mr. Watson has assumed that in the first line the poet is bidding 'goodnight' not to a dead friend, real or imagined, but to himself, and has concluded that the poem was written in anticipation of suicide—'he was led, as a single short poem testifies, not only to contemplate the interception of death but to welcome its abysmal finality.'

Having chosen so to interpret the poem, the biographer has to find an event in the poet's life capable of 'precipitating' it. Can it have been (he asks) the news of a serious illness of the poet's father? or the recollection (after twelve years) of his mother's death? Neither seems to Mr. Watson an adequate explanation of this suicidal impulse. Can it, then, have been some misunderstanding or estrangement between himself and Jackson? There is nothing to show that anything of the sort occurred; and Mr. Watson is thus driven to his conclusion that Housman's 'exquisite threnody' was 'precipitated' by his discovery of the nature of his feelings for his friend.

So Mr. Watson founds his theory upon an arbitrary interpretation of 'Parta Quies', linked with a misconception of the poet's psychology. Even the dating upon which he bases the hypothesis is insecure. He presents the poem as 'solid evidence' that the 'hideous discovery' was made 'sometime in 1881 but preceding the examination for Greats', during Housman's 'penultimate months at Oxford'. But contributions to the March number of *Waifs and Strays* (the number in which the poem appeared) had to be sent in within a fortnight of the beginning of Hilary Term, which in 1881 began on 14 January. The poem must therefore have been sent in before the end of January, and the event that 'precipitated' it cannot have occurred during Housman's last, or even his penultimate, term at Oxford.

Better evidence was to hand if Mr. Watson had cared to use it. Among Housman's posthumously published poems is one in which he looks back on the hopeful period of his youth: 'When I was young,' he wrote,

> *May stuck the land with wickets:*
> *For all the eye could tell,*
> *The world went well.*

Housman Obscured

Yet well, God knows, it went not,
God knows, it went awry;
For me one flowery Maytime
It went so ill that I
Designed to die.

That is evidence, if one wants it—it would be rash to call it 'solid evidence', but it has the ring of authenticity—that something went very wrong for Housman—indeed, that he came near to suicide—in the month of May one year when he was young. In 1881, Greats began on 28 May. Perhaps this 'Maytime' misfortune, whatever it may have been, was the cause of Housman's disastrous performance in Greats at the end of that month; perhaps (and this seems more likely) his failure in Greats was itself the misfortune he refers to; in either alternative, it occurred after the publication of *Waifs and Strays* in March, and cannot have given rise to the 'exquisite threnody'.

Clearly the greatest circumspection and reserve is needed if we are to draw biographical conclusions from such uncertain evidence. Mr. Watson suffers from no such inhibition: he is ever ready with what he calls 'an obvious biographical interpretation' of poems which, as Housman's notebooks show, he began to compose years after the happening of the events to which the biographer would refer them—events with which they have no demonstrable, and sometimes even no probable connexion.

When Mr. Watson is not restrained by evidence, his imagination ranges more freely, and we are given a series of pictures of the state of Housman's emotions which have no warrant other than the author's conviction that this is how Housman ought to have felt. Thus, when Jackson has departed for India:

'With the knowledge that comes only from a trial of the spirit, [Housman] discovered in those early months of 1888 how fatally, in spite of all his efforts to detach himself, he was still subject to whatever torments and upheavals Jackson might be disposed to inflict. . . . [His] thoughts often reverted, under the wet skies of Hampstead, to his old penchant for astronomy. . . . Magnificently aloof, the stars hung there as if to remind him that his throbbing consciousness would soon be extinguished in "a foolscap of eternal shade"; and conversely that here on "the turning globe" he was, like Empedocles, governed by some unfathomable system which allotted to each his own ultimate share of pain and pleasure. Tormented by such metaphysical quandaries, &c., &c.'

Later, but while Housman was still at University College (referred to by Mr. Watson as 'the crepuscular purlieus of Gower Street'), we read that Jackson (now married and Principal of a College in Karachi) 'inadvertently retained the power to cast a spell over Housman's life. But with its roots fastened to his character like barnacles, the spell had outlasted its potency, and was now perversely sustained by his determination not only to repel the encroachment of some alternative experience, but to draw from the bitter dregs of his past an irrefutable lesson.'

Finally, in 1911, soon after Housman had arrived at Cambridge (with its 'palatial Renaissance courtyards and spellbound Gothic vistas' by 'the peaceful Cam'), news reached him that Jackson was to return from India to spend his retirement not in England but in British Columbia.

'Certainly [says Mr. Watson] the ultimate effects of his choice were not lost upon Housman, whose sequestered academic life now held no prospect of that Odyssean culmination of which, hitherto, he could indulge the patient hope; and suffering this disappointment in the hour of his triumph, he was not only listless with regret for what-might-have-been, but more prone to withdraw, in his first winter at Cambridge, from the pleasures that were left to him.'

'Well!' one is tempted to exclaim, after reading pages of biographical speculation such as this, 'that, or something like it, may have been the case. But could we not be told about it in less confident and highly coloured language?'

Mr. Watson dismisses briefly the quarter of a century (1911–36) during which Housman lived in Cambridge. 'The formidable scholar and ruthless pedant, the emendator of Manilius and the Kennedy Professor of Latin,' he says, 'are not the subject of this book.' That sentence reveals a fundamental defect in Housman's biographer. It is not merely a question of not knowing Greek and Latin. In his preface, Mr. Watson thanks a friend for 'enlarging his grasp' of those languages—an enlargement which, however, has not saved him from writing of 'Lucullian repasts', of 'this erotica', 'that juvenilia', and 'this invidious marginalia'; from misquoting and twice mistranslating, at key points, the Latin lines which Housman addressed to Jackson; or from referring to Manilius's *Astronomica* as an epic. Such solecisms do not matter very much; what does matter is that Mr. Watson has no clear idea of what it was that engaged the energies of Housman's mind, of the nature of his intellectual gifts and his intellectual passion, of what it meant to him to be a scholar. He writes him off with a fresh batch of clichés as a 'choleric pedant', and a 'crabbed scholar', 'ageing into tetchiness and hebetude', engaged in 'pallid labours' and 'engulfed in professorial quirks', who 'continued to scale the peaks of scholarship but with an air of increasing hostility and rancour'. Of what it means to edit a classical text he evidently has no conception whatever. At one point he actually taints ignorance with bad taste by treating *Praefanda*, a learned paper on what he archly calls 'naughty Latinisms' as a 'joke' on Housman's part, which he says must have 'gleefully occupied him for many summers'. Irony there was, no doubt, in Housman's precise and detached treatment of Martial's intricate and obscure obscenities; Mr. Watson sees the article simply as a 'lewd gesture' in which Housman indulged with 'venerable gusto'.

If the editor of Manilius lies outside the range of Mr. Watson's comprehension, so too does the author of *A Shropshire Lad*. He recognizes Housman's debt to Heine, 'the volatile Jewish poet—a dashing, intemperate renegade whose stormy and improvident life bore no resemblance to that of his staid Victorian admirer'; and to the authors of the Border Ballads—'the anonymous bards who poured into their rudimentary moulds a literature that ranged from *Chevy Chase* to *Clerk Saunders*'—ballads which (in Mr. Watson's characteristic metaphor) 'preserved, as in the untarnished miniatures of some Book of Hours, the domestic scenes as well as the popular legends, the distilled composite experience of medieval country life'.

[143]

Housman Obscured

He realizes that poetry was for Housman, as he himself described it, a 'morbid secretion' which he extruded half-unconsciously, half-reluctantly, in response to some intolerable inner pressure. But he can give no coherent account of the (still unexplained) 'continuous excitement' under which a great part of *A Shropshire Lad* was composed in the early months of 1895, and this is what he has to say about the period of silence which followed the publication of that volume (when 'Housman's little book sank close to oblivion, while a grim silence descended upon his prostrate muse'):

'The course of public events offered him a gamut of congenial subject matter. . . . United in spirit with the young men who slept on desolate colonial battlefields, and perhaps also visited by those stabs of remorse which afflict the non-combatant in such a context, Housman was admirably fitted, it would have seemed, to become the valedictorian of an age whose anxious last phase coincided with the highest reach of his own sensibilities. A poet already expert in the technical manipulation of his art, he could have scarcely failed to meet, if his creative impulse had been strong enough, the challenge of this opportunity. . . . But neither intensity of feeling nor vigour of mind availed to release that subsconscious mechanism which governed the ebb and flow of his poetry; so that when the historic hour struck, Housman was forced to busy himself, not with a surging Ode upon the Death of Queen Victoria, but with the minute pedestrian study of Manilius.'

Housman's creative activity, we know, was not always subject to his conscious control; but he would surely have been surprised if his subconscious had presented him with a surging ode on the death of Queen Victoria.

Le style, c'est l'homme même : Mr. Watson's style evidently takes shape from his conception of the subject matter; it is impossible to distinguish the way he writes about his subject from the way he thinks about it. Moreover, his method of presentation is such that it is difficult to be sure, at almost any moment, whether what he tells us is proved fact or simply surmise. But the real weakness of his book goes deeper; when one has sifted fact from metaphor, and fact (or reasonable inference) from mere conjecture, what remains is nothing but the familiar fragmentary story. The truth that lies at the bottom of Mr. Watson's treacle-well is not new: the little that we can be sure of—the 'long and sure-set liking', the unanswered passion—is already there in the poems and in the pages of Mr. Gow and of Mr. Laurence Housman. Everything that Mr. Watson adds is open to question; he has tried in vain to atone for uncertainty of outline in his picture by heightening its colours. And everything that was a problem remains a problem: the failure in the Schools, the 'continuous excitement' in 1895, the relation between individual poems and the poet's actual experience. The temptation to fill in the gaps is no doubt a strong one, but the subject is not one that lends itself to imaginative reconstruction; for one thing, it is too near in time—we know at once too much and too little about it. The imaginary portrait is a legitimate form of literature—it is even, perhaps, a legitimate form of history, as Mme Yourcenar has shown in her *Memoirs of Hadrian*—but it can hardly be written with success except about the distant past, and it requires learning and genius for its execution. Even if Mr. Watson had been a shrewder critic he would not have succeeded in the task he set himself; but then, if he had been a shrewder critic, would he ever have embarked upon it?

Barrie and Himself[1]

'I wonder you have not been found out before as one of the most beautiful writers of the English language that ever lived': that, from George Moore, was high praise; it was to Barrie, after reading this book, that he wrote it. The tribute was not undeserved. Barrie could not help writing beautifully; his works are seductive quite as much (though their readers do not always recognize it) by reason of the limpidity of his prose as by reason of the strength of his personality. Sometimes, for a blessed interval, he allows that personality a rest, and the quality of his writing can then be judged in abstraction. It has all the Addisonian virtues: lucidity, an easy flow, an unerring choice of words, the right pitch, the right weight—Barrie could always say just what he wanted to say in just the tone of voice that he intended. Authors who can write like that will never lack readers, provided that they have something to say. Something to say—that, alas! was where Barrie was deficient.

It is here that comparison with another strongly personal writer is instructive. Like Barrie, Kipling used the English language as a master; unlike Barrie, Kipling had a personality which even his greatest admirers could find unattractive. But Kipling's observation was as comprehensive, his creative imagination was as prolific, as Barrie's were limited and sterile. Kipling found his material everywhere, and the English language was his medium for conveying to his readers a whole store of accumulated riches. So it is that however little you like Kipling, you cannot but admire him, and nine-tenths of the time you forget your dislike in your admiration. Barrie, on the other hand, had nothing to give us but his personality. You either like him and his writings, therefore, or you do not, and there is an end of it. His prose is simply a medium for conveying himself; when

[1] A review of *The Greenwood Hat*, by J. M. Barrie, 1937.

[146]

his personality is in abeyance, so is his power. His plays are perhaps an exception to this generalization: for while it is true that to those who read them his personality oozes through the chinks afforded by the confidential stage directions, when they are performed they have an effectiveness that is independent of his personal impress, though they do bear that impress strongly.

The Greenwood Hat—the title is wholly misleading in the suggestion it conveys of Robin Hood—consists of a number of essays contributed to the *St. James's Gazette* in Barrie's very earliest days as a journalist, when Frederick Greenwood was its editor. Some years before his death, Barrie made a selection of these papers and reprinted them privately with retrospective comments of his own.

The *St. James's* essays are Barrie at his best. They are light effusions, belonging obviously to the world of journalism in which Stevenson, Andrew Lang, Austin Dobson (all of them accomplished writers) were influential. This kind of writing has 'gone out' since the war, except in the hands of Mr. Beerbohm, whose insight, depth, and sureness of touch can make even trifles enduring. Barrie had not yet developed that *alter ego* with which he played at hide-and-seek throughout his later works, and in these essays he ranges over a variety of topics incognito. Several of these papers—those, for instance, on an imaginary first novel, on Ladies at Cricket, on a schoolboy home for the holidays, and his parody of Sandford and Merton—are amusing enough. But they are slight, and would hardly have been worth reprinting but for the reminiscential passages that accompany each essay. In these, the Barrie of 1930 looks back on the Barrie of the 1880s. No occupation could have been more congenial; it is Barrie inviting us to join Barrie in observing Barrie: once it was Maconochie; now it is 'Mr. Anon'. He is dismissed, at the close, with affectionate archness, in the phrase: 'Begone, sweet Anon, begone', having been introduced as follows:

'Let us survey our hero as he sits awake in a corner of his railway compartment, well aware that the end of it must be to perch, or to let go, like a bat in the darkness behind the shutter. He has a suspicious eye, poor gomeril, for any fellow-traveller who is civil to him. He is gauche and inarticulate, and as thin as a pencil but not so long (and is going to be thinner). Expression, an uncomfortable blank. Wears thick boots (with nails in them), which he will polish specially for social functions. Carries on his person a silver watch bought for him by his father from a pedlar on fourteenth birthday (that was a day). Carries it still, No. 57841. Has no complete dress-suit in his wooden box, but can look every inch as if attired in such when backed against a wall. Manners, full of nails like his boots. Ladies have decided that he is of no account, and he already knows this and has private anguish thereanent. Hates sentiment as a slave may hate his master.'

The skill with which this picture is drawn is undeniable; but that a man should be on such affectionate terms with himself, even after so long an interval of years, itself gives rise to an uncomfortable feeling; and in the public display of that affection there is something positively unbecoming. It is not that any fault is to be found with the personality itself. In private life Barrie's qualities may have been irresistible—it is his attitude on paper that gives offence. He comes too near; compelling a violation at once of the reader's privacy and of his own. A Frenchman said of Barrie that his style was a succession of blows beneath the belt; but it is nothing so hostile as a blow, it is a caress, and it has all the power of a caress to charm and to repel.

Thousands have been charmed by that caress, accepting the intimacy he proffered and taking him to their hearts, and for the last quarter of a century he must have been one of the three or four most popular 'literary' authors writing English. There is no reason why his popularity should wane, for it was not founded on any temporary appeal in the subjects that he wrote about or in the forms in which he wrote. His plays, perhaps, will not keep the stage for long, but they were written just as much for drawing-room reading as for performance, and as long as there are drawing-rooms they will be read.

There is no question what company of authors he belongs to; it is the company of Lamb, of Stevenson, of Goldsmith: when he summons up the ghosts of the Adelphi it is Charles Lamb who is 'of all my visitors the most desired', and it is Lamb whom of all authors he resembles most. Both were masters of the craft of writing; both were versatile; both unrivalled in the lightness of their touch; both had a real humorous power, yet neither could ever learn that in order to be amusing it is not necessary to be whimsical. 'Mr. Anon' is simply Elia *redivivus*, and doubtless like Elia he will exercise the same fascination over posterity that he exercised over his contemporaries.

Barrie's reputation and his achievement present a curious problem, and it is difficult to know whether it is an aesthetic problem or a moral one. He was, it must be admitted, a consummate artist, but he would repudiate any claim to admiration on that score. Indeed, those who care for that combination of form and substance in which the art of literature consists will find little to care for in his work. It is the lovers of personalities on paper that are his natural admirers; yet his artistic presentation of his personality is the very thing that, to the discriminating, throws an air of something like indecency over all his work.

The End of Casement[1]

'When I landed in Ireland that morning (about 3 a.m.), swamped and swimming ashore on an unknown strand, I was happy for the first time for over a year. Although I knew that this fate waited on me, I was for one brief spell happy and smiling once more. I cannot tell you what I felt. The sandhills were full of skylarks, rising in the dawn, the first I had heard for years—the first sound I heard was their song as I waded in through the breakers, and they kept rising all the time up to the old rath at Curraghane, where I stayed and sent the others on, and all around were primroses and violets and the singing of the skylarks in the air, and I was back in Ireland again. As the day grew brighter I was quite happy, for I felt all the time that it was God's will that I was there.'

That is Casement as his friends—and all but the bitterest, surely, of his enemies—would wish to think of him: Casement in rare moments of stress or exaltation; romantic, selfless, dedicated, a man of noble spirit and of single mind. It was at the 'old rath', a few hours later, that he was taken prisoner, and from Curraghane was but a step to Pentonville, where, not long before his execution, he wrote those words. Is the portrait they suggest a true one? Was that the real Casement? 'One of them,' it seems, must be the answer; 'one among others.'

To those others the diaries now published introduce us. There is Casement the consular official, the Foreign Office representative; tall, bronzed, athletic, with something Spanish in his dark good looks; pacing tropical verandas, impatient of official interference; striding

[1] A review of *The Black Diaries*, edited by P. Singleton-Gates and M. Girodias, 1960.

[150]

off into the Congo forests with a couple of bulldogs at his heels; trudging the jungle tracks in the Amazon with the Indian rubber-convoy, listening to their tales of suffering, cross-examining their persecutors, sitting up all night among the mosquitoes to scribble his dispatches; resolute in his determination to extirpate an evil.

That is a real Casement, too. And that same Casement can be met also on leave in London; putting up at lodgings in Philbeach Gardens, dining alone at the Comedy Restaurant, playing billiards at the club; going to dine with Conan Doyle and afterwards to see *The Speckled Band*, or Irving at the Lyceum; running down to the country to spend the day with Conrad, with Morel, with Scawen Blunt; chuckling over the *Irish R.M.* in his hotel bedroom; reading Marie Corelli in the train; writing fourth-rate sentimental verses:

> *Love is the ocean's purple.*
> *Love is the mountain's crest.*
> *Love is the Golden Eagle*
> *That hither builds his nest—*

Casement having a 'splendid talk' on 'Anti-Slavery' with Noel Buxton; complaining of Foreign Office delays and stupidities—all, it seems, aimed (for no apparent reason) at himself—a querulous, restless, rootless figure; a man of moody enthusiasms and facile reactions, ready to lend himself to movements and to causes, but with no depth of passion or distinction of taste in art or letters or personal relationships.

Then there was Casement the Irish patriot—known as such only to a small circle of his acquaintance, to Mrs. Stopford Green, to Bulmer Hobson, to the leaders of the Irish Volunteers; the Casement who contributed political harangues to *The Ulster Guardian, The Freeman's Journal, The Irish Independent*; who 'dreamed and planned', in the heart of the Amazon forests, 'a great Irish romance of the future'; who gave up his London club to devote his subscription to a Gaelic Training College in Munster; who, seeing in England's crisis Ireland's opportunity, went to Germany when war broke out to recruit an 'Irish Brigade' for the Cause.

We see this Casement in the Wilhelmstrasse in 1915, 'on a big sofa, in this centre of policy of the German Empire', with 'no regrets, no fears—well, yes, some regrets, but no fears'; we see him at Limburg Lahn, trying to bribe the unhappy prisoners with visions of an Ireland freed by their efforts from the tyrant, and retreating before their indignation, booed, hissed, assaulted—'swinging his umbrella to cover his retreat'—saved from their violence only by the Prussian escort provided for him 'by a nation' (in F.E.'s delightful phrase) 'which thinks of everything'. We watch him losing the confidence of his Irish-American employers; losing faith, in his turn, in his German hosts; losing his nerve, too, at Sassnitz; breaking down before Countess Blücher; sick in mind and body, desperate and disillusioned; till, committed to a mission that he felt to be foredoomed to failure, he stumbled ashore at dawn on that Good Friday at the 'old rath' at Curraghane, with the larks singing in the sky above him, and knew, for the last time, a moment's happiness.

But there was yet another Casement: Casement incognito, on the loose, in London, in Belfast, on board ship, in Lisbon, or São Paulo or Buenos Aires; Casement in Madeira, prowling round the Alameda Gardens; at Para, perambulating his hunting-grounds in the 'big Square' or Baptista Campos; Casement hanging round the barracks at Manaos, eyeing the natives on the quayside at La Chorrera; waiting in vain for Ignacio in the Square at Iquitos, or not in vain for Agostinho outside the casino at Funchal; Casement with Ramon in the Zoo at Buenos Aires or 'in the Bosquet afterwards'; Casement nearer home, keeping a rendezvous with 'Albert' or 'Welsh Will' at the Marble Arch, or engaging a room for himself and the enigmatic but energetic Millar at the Northern Counties Hotel in Belfast—Casement morning, noon, and night with one preoccupation: a devotee for whom at every encounter the presiding deity was Priapus. That picture—and it is a self-portrait, drawn with no lack of lubricious detail—is that, too, authentic? Is *that* the real Casement? 'That is another of them' must be the answer.

The Black Diaries, in which all these figures are to be met, the last-mentioned for the first time, was printed in the United States and published in Paris by the Olympia Press of Mr. Maurice Girodias (to whom the world is indebted also for *Lolita, An Adult's Story, Lust,* and *Ladies at Night*); it appears in England in a 'special' edition of 2,000 copies which duplicates the American edition and omits one of the three diaries (that which covers 1911) included in the Paris issue. The volume is riddled with misprints and more serious blunders, thrown together without an index, deficient in maps and tastelessly illustrated; and the politico-historico-biographical setting provided for the diaries by the editors is so crudely written and so distorted by anti-English bias as to be unworthy of serious notice.

Nonetheless, *The Black Diaries* is an important book, both for students of history and for students of human nature. Here (reprinted, presumably, from Command Papers) are Casement's reports on his investigations in the Congo in 1903 and in the Putumayo in 1910; and facing them on the opposite pages, the texts of the diaries that he kept during those same years. These texts are derived from typescripts made in Scotland Yard at the time of the trial and handed to one of the editors in 1922 by 'a person of some authority in London'. The diaries themselves are preserved in the Public Record Office, together with other note-books used as diaries by Casement in 1903 and 1911; comparison with these originals confirms that their contents are on the whole faithfully recorded in the printed text.

The publication of these texts has set at rest one question, if it revives or raises others. It has settled the question whether the diaries are genuine, but it will certainly stimulate curiosity about the use that was made of them by the authorities at the time of Casement's trial, and it will prompt, in the new light thrown on Casement's conduct, the question whether he received justice at the hands of the English, and what should be the verdict of history upon him.

It was at the time of Casement's trial in the summer of 1916 that rumours first reached the Press and the public that diaries containing records of his indulgence in homosexual practices had been found by the police in his London lodgings. No Irish patriot could admit such a slur upon a name over which the martyr's halo was already poised, and the word went round that the diaries were forgeries—fabricated by the British Government, or their agents, in order to blacken Casement's reputation. Suspicion was turned to

certainty in the minds of many by the persistent refusal of the authorities, during the succeeding half-century, to make any admissions
concerning the contents, or even the existence, of these documents:
the Government, then, had something to hide; the diaries *must* be
forged. So there grew up a whole body of literature, written largely,
it seems, by Irish medical men, seeking to establish with almost
Baconian ingenuity the hypothesis of forgery; *The Forged Casement
Diaries*, by Dr. W. J. Maloney; *The Life and Times of Roger Casement*,
by Dr. H. O. Mackey; *The Accusing Ghost or Justice for Casement*, by
Alfred Noyes. No theory was too fantastic, no charge against the
English authorities too monstrous, for these enthusiasts, and much
of what they wrote is mere scurrility. But the theme was made
memorable by a nobler pen:

> *Afraid they might be beaten*
> *Before the bench of Time*
> *They turned a trick by forgery*
> *And blackened his good name—*

and Yeats's evocation of 'the ghost of Roger Casement' has persuaded
many who, where English villainy is suggested, are prone to mistake
rhetoric for evidence.

To support the campaign against the English various theories were
advanced: either the whole thing was a fabrication (concocted, one
must suppose, before Casement's capture, on the off-chance of its
being of use if ever he fell into English hands): or else the 'black'
passages were invented and inserted into diaries themselves genuine;
or else the Government passed off as Casement's diaries documents
which were either transcripts by him of the diaries of Normand, a
Peruvian blackguard whom he was seeking to expose, or memoranda
that he made of evidence supplied to him concerning the sexual habits
of the Amazonian Indians.

The texts now printed scatter all such theories to the winds. Faced
with this voluminous and detailed daily record of Casement's travels
in three continents, the accuracy of which at a number of points is
confirmed by independent sources, not even the most fanatical of his
apologists (such as Dr. Mackey in a recent pamphlet *I Accuse*) is bold
enough to suggest that the whole text is invented. Attack is

concentrated on the 'black' entries. But these themselves record—with names, dates, addresses and more personal particulars—sexual experiences not only in South America but in Africa, in Ireland, in London, on board ship; they cannot be transcripts of a Peruvian's diary, any more than they can be anthropological memoranda concerning native practices.

And these 'black' entries are so inextricably interwoven with innocent matter that they cannot be explained as subsequent insertions into an existing text. To give but one illustration: the 'black' matter includes scores of entries recording payments (e.g. to 'Welsh Will', to Agostinho, to Carlos Costa, to 'Clubfoot') which leave no doubt about the kind of services that were being paid for; at more than one point such figures recur (together with figures relating to innocent expenditure) in comprehensive accounts that carry their genuineness upon their face. (These payments, incidentally, afford perhaps the clearest refutation—there are others—of the theory that the sexual adventures chronicled in the diaries were not actual experiences but day-dreams—the wish-fulfilments of a frustrated man.)

Such entries as these confirm almost to demonstration, the genuineness of the suspected passages; equally convincing, though impossible to convey by isolated quotation, is the impression of unity given by the diaries as a whole, 'black' and innocent passages alike: this is not the invention of some Home Office or Intelligence official, it is the diary of a real person—the strange production, certainly, of a strange man, but a record unmistakably authentic.

If further confirmation be needed, the actual documents in the Record Office provide it. Scribbled in the jungle, on board ship, in hotel bedrooms, in differing inks, sometimes in pencil, with frequent interlineations and insertions—they are themselves as remarkable as the texts that they contain; but no one who scrutinizes them in an impartial frame of mind can doubt that they are what they lay claim to be. Even Dr. Mackey, having examined them, does not suggest that the body of the text is not in Casement's hand. And here again the interweaving of 'black' matter with matter undoubtedly from Casement's pen is fatal to the hypothesis of his innocence. Indeed, no serious critic who has read the text or examined the documents believes in it any longer.

The End of Casement

Attack has of necessity been diverted from the genuineness of the diaries and aimed instead at the use that was made of them. For there is no doubt that at the time of Casement's trial the fact that he had kept such diaries was divulged, and extracts from them were copied and shown to persons capable of influencing opinion in Britain and the United States. It hardly seems possible now to discover with any precision how widely these copies were circulated and who authorized their circulation, and perhaps these questions are no longer important. What is important, if judgment is to be passed in the matter, is to know why the thing was done, and what was its effect.

On that, the almost universal view (which still prevails) is that the diaries were used, and used successfully, in order to ensure that Casement should be hanged. The Cabinet, it is said, 'in their hatred of Casement' and 'for the brief pleasure of hanging him' used them 'to prevent any agitation mounting for a reprieve'; this is the charge advanced by the editors of *The Black Diaries*. Since it is made the basis of bitter attacks upon the morality of the Cabinet of the day, and since the question is one of some historical interest if not importance, it deserves to be examined carefully. Such examination shows strikingly how truth can be turned inside out in little more than a generation.

So far from wishing to hang Casement, the Government had every reason to look for a pretext on which to spare his life. The outcome of the war, then trembling in the balance, might well depend upon America's entry into it; American opinion was adverse to England's treatment of Ireland and sensitive to Irish pressure: to make Casement an Irish martyr might mean the loss of the vital ally. This was a constant anxiety of the Government at the time; the necessity of conciliating American opinion was being pressed upon them by Spring Rice, our ambassador in Washington, and it was urged after Casement's conviction as a reason for reprieving him by characters as diverse as the Archbishop of Canterbury and Bernard Shaw.

Public opinion at home pulled strongly in the other direction: the gutter Press was crying out for the traitor's execution, and even the fair-minded might well see no ground for granting to him the clemency denied to the rebel leaders who had been shot out of hand not many weeks before.

The End of Casement

In this dilemma, the diaries may have seemed to present to the Government a loophole of escape. So extravagant are the excesses they record, so extraordinary is the obsession they bear witness to, that they might well be thought to be (as some of Casement's apologists still think them) the product of a disordered and unbalanced mind. Might they not afford ground for a reprieve, if not for an acquittal, on grounds of insanity?

In fact, the diaries were offered to the defence at Casement's trial with this possibility in view: that is the evidence of Casement's counsel; 'Smith did his best to get me to plead guilty but insane,' said Serjeant Sullivan, adding that F. E. Smith, who (prosecuting, as Attorney-General) made the offer of the diaries, was furious when it was refused. Smith's anger may well have been due to disappointment at the frustration of a double aim: a verdict of 'Guilty but insane' would at once have saved Casement's life and robbed him of the martyr's crown.

Sullivan was no doubt right in refusing to look at the diaries, which could not really have assisted him in the defence. They might, nonetheless, have afforded grounds for a reprieve, and this view was pressed upon the Cabinet, after Casement's appeal had been dismissed, by Randall Davidson, as Bishop Bell recounts in his Life of the Archbishop: 'Though not technically (according to experts) a man out of his mind, he is shown to have been mentally and morally unhinged. In these complicated circumstances,' suggested the Archbishop, the Cabinet might say 'we believe that the more sane and fair course is . . . to commute the sentence.' They may well have been fortified in resistance to such pleading by a memorandum of Sir Ernley Blackwell, the legal adviser to the Home Office, who correctly pointed out that Casement was 'very far removed from anything that could properly be described as insanity' and that his sexual excesses had not 'any relevance in consideration of his crime'.

To refuse a reprieve was no easy decision, and one which was not reached, it is said, without a vote (the single member of that Cabinet who survives cannot, of course, disclose what passed). Public opinion abroad and at home pulled in opposite directions; expediency sided with mercy; but in the absence of any legal ground for clemency, and with the recent Dublin executions no doubt in mind, Ministers took the harder course. There is no reason to challenge the summing-up of Asquith's biographers:

'The Cabinet considered the question . . . on at least three occasions with evident anxiety to discover a loophole if one could be found. The only possible loophole was a certificate of insanity which no competent medical authority would sign. Failing this Ministers felt it impossible to reprieve the ring-leader when thirteen of his followers had suffered the extreme penalty.'

So much for the suggestion that the Cabinet used the diaries to 'prevent' the reprieve that they would in fact have been only too glad to recommend; indeed, had they really been set upon Casement's execution they would hardly have been deterred by counting, or by weighing, the names appended to petitions for clemency. What they feared was the potency of the legend that might spring from Casement's grave to ruin England and the Allies; it was to prevent the growth of that legend that the diaries were employed. Here again the Cabinet seems to have listened to the advice of Blackwell, who wrote, after the appeal had been dismissed, 'So far as I can judge it would be far wiser, from every point of view, to allow the law to take its course and, by judicious means, to use the diaries to prevent Casement attaining martyrdom'—they were to be used, it will be noted, not in order to ensure his execution but in order to counter its possible effects.

Whether the decision to make this use of these extracts was taken at Cabinet level is uncertain; the fact that they were so used is indisputable, and has brought bitter attacks upon the British Government. The attack has come usually from those who supposed that the diaries were forged in order to 'get Casement hanged'; it was to this view of the case that Yeats applied the saying of the old Fenian: 'There are things a man must not do even to save a nation.' But even if all dishonesty is out of the question, the decision—to use a man's private diaries in order to damage his posthumous reputation—cannot have been an easy one to take; may one ever do even a little evil in order that much good may come of it? The moral quality of the decision, however, cannot be judged without considering its circumstances and the frame of mind and motives of those who took it.

As for the circumstances, they could hardly have been more compelling: the denial, or even the postponement, of American aid to Britain might spell the ruin of that civilization for which men were dying by hundreds every day. It is difficult to blame those responsible if they felt that a limited circulation of an (after all) authentic document was justifiable where so vast a national, and more than national, interest was at stake.

Even if the circumstances justified the decision, those who took it would have been open to grave attack had they been actuated in any measure by vindictiveness. It does not appear that there is evidence to support such a charge, at any rate as regards members of the Cabinet. If any Minister might seem liable to that suspicion, it would surely be the figure who, having served the Ulster Volunteers as Galloper Smith, led for the prosecution at Casement's trial as Attorney-General; and critics have been reckless in their attacks upon 'F.E.', charging him with 'hatred and dishonesty' in his conduct of the prosecution, and accusing him of having shown round the diaries to please the prurient, or simply in order to blacken the character of his old enemy. The proceedings at the trial have been published for the world to see, and 'carefully as one may search the record of the case, it is impossible' (in the words of Mr. René Mac-Coll, whose *Life* is the best—indeed, one may say the only adequate —biography of Casement) 'to find anything to show that Smith behaved in an unfair or incorrect manner'. H. W. Nevinson, who proved both his courage and his devotion to Casement by shaking hands with the prisoner in the dock, had no fault to find in Smith's closing speech save its 'Oxford accent'; and Sullivan himself, in a letter written at the end of the case and recently printed in Lord Birkenhead's biography of his father, thanked the Attorney-General for the 'kindness and consideration' he had shown to the defence and referred to his 'desire to be chivalrous and generous to the weaker side'. The trial, he added, was a proceeding 'of which you and your countrymen may well be proud. It was a splendid demonstration of the manner in which justice should be administered'.

As for allegations that F.E. made improper use of the diaries, another piece of contemporary evidence, first printed in Lord Birkenhead's biography, throws a vivid light on his, and his colleagues', attitude in the matter. On the last day of the trial (29 June) Smith wrote to Edward Grey saying that he was told that the Foreign Office had photographed or proposed to photograph 'portions of Casement's diary with a view to showing them to various people so as to influence opinion'. Evidently the suggestion was new to him; his reaction to it was immediate: 'It is I think,' he wrote, 'rather a ghoulish proposal.' Grey in reply declared that he had not heard of the proposal and did not approve of it, and undertook that it should not be proceeded with as far as the Foreign Office was concerned 'without the authority of the Cabinet, to whom I think such proceedings would be most disagreeable'. These are spontaneous letters written at the time, and not written for publication; plainly, if the Cabinet did take this disagreeable decision, they took it in a spirit very different from that imputed to them by their critics.

In the light of this, the Government's continued insistence on keeping the diaries secret can be better understood: so far from concealing evidence of their own forgery, they were prepared to suffer that imputation undeservedly rather than inflict further damage on Casement's good name when no overriding purpose was any longer to be served.

This attitude accorded with the wishes of those of Casement's countrymen who knew the truth. On this matter also Lord Birkenhead provides fresh evidence in his biography, printing a memorandum preserved in the National Library of Ireland in which Eamon Duggan declared that:

'Some one who had surreptitious recourse to the diary wrote a book —a life of Casement, I think—making public the diary. At the request of certain people here (in Dublin) who didn't wish the memory of Casement or anyone associated with 1916 reviled, Birkenhead went to the publishers (who happened to be, because of his position [he was by now Lord Chancellor] amenable to the suggestion that he made to them) with the result that the book was not published.'

This shows clearly enough that at that later date, as in 1916, the attitude of Birkenhead was the reverse of vindictive, and it would be surprising if such men as Grey or Asquith or Buckmaster had been less scrupulous than he.

From Casement's 'Right Honourable accusers' (to borrow his own satirical phrase) one returns to the prisoner himself. Did he receive justice at their hands, legally, or in the larger sense? And how will these new revelations of his character and conduct affect the world's final estimate of the man?

As a matter of law, in spite of the arguments gallantly and skilfully deployed by Serjeant Sullivan and the efforts of editors of the diaries to wrest a new meaning out of the wording of the treason Statute—could acts committed 'without the realm' amount to treason?—there can be no doubt but that the verdict was a right one. The *dicta* of Coke, of Hale, of Hawkins, and more recent judicial interpretations of the Act put the matter beyond dispute.

And even if the construction of the Statute for which Sullivan contended had been sound, justice would surely have been mocked if Casement had been saved 'by a comma'—for it is no less a mockery of justice that a man should owe his acquittal than that he should owe his condemnation to the faulty wording or punctuation of an Act. If the things that Casement did in Germany had not been covered by the treason Statute simply because it failed to reach outside the realm, then it would have been high time to amend it so as to include them.

It was a pity that such points were taken on Casement's behalf, but it was a greater pity still that he instructed his defenders to challenge the evidence about his activities and intentions in Germany, and to claim that he was recruiting the Irish Brigade only for service after the German war was over. That claim was easily refuted—why, if it was true, did the prisoners meet his proposals with such indignant contempt?—and in suggesting that he was a traitor neither in fact nor in law Casement was denying what in his better moments he would have regarded as his better self. Of course he was a traitor, and he should have gloried in it.

For Casement's bitter hatred of England was of long standing and not, as F. E. Smith supposed, a sudden and a recent growth. It was the Boer War, he tells us, that turned him first against the country he was serving. Already in 1907 he was quoting Michael Davitt with approval: 'The idea of being ruled by Englishmen is to me the chief agony of existence. They are a nation without faith, truth, or conscience.' He thought that the Irishman's wrongs called more urgently for redress than the African's: 'Nothing could destroy or efface the ineffaceable negro—his ways, his colour, his mind, his stature and all that make him the negro. . . . In the case of Ireland—how different. It is now or never indeed.' That was in 1905. Ten years later, the war gave Ireland her opportunity; in August 1914, he writes from New York: 'If Germany wins through against this gang of criminals, hope shall spring again'; his 'heart bleeds' for 'poor Germany'; ' "God save Germany" I pray night and day.' Arrived in Berlin, 'My country,' he exclaims, 'can only gain from my treason.' 'I shall have given more to Ireland,' he writes, 'by one bold deed of open treason than Redmond and Company after years of talk and spouting. . . . Those men have killed England with their mouth time and again—I am going to hit her with my clenched hand.'

It was not for the man who wrote those words, and meant them from his heart, to prevaricate in Court about the definition of treason, to complain about the antiquity of the Statute under which he was convicted, or to pretend that his Irish Brigade was not intended to help Germany in her struggle against the common foe.

It is not only by the criteria of the lawyer and the moralist that Casement's fate must be deemed a just one; there was about it also a justice truly poetic, for it gave to his disordered career a climax that made a design of the whole. Nothing in his life became him like the leaving of it; acquittal or reprieve would have denied it the dignity of tragedy. To have stepped free out of the Old Bailey would have been to add to his career an element all of a piece with the accepted knighthood, an anticlimax more ignominious than the fiasco on Banna Strand. To have been removed to Broadmoor, on the hollow pretext of insanity, would have been to exchange tragedy for farce—and a farce with a deferred epilogue that could hardly, however things went, have been anything but wretched. What would life have had to offer to the ageing Casement on his ultimate release? He might have grown hard—'withered old and skeleton-gaunt, an image of

[his] politics'; or (worse fate) he might have grown soft, the fine figure of his early manhood declining entirely into the epicene Casement known of old to Agostinho. Either way, it was better to die in mid-career, 'changed, changed utterly' by martyrdom.

There is yet another kind of justice—the justice dispensed not by judges or moralists, nor yet by dramatists, but by historians. For the historian's method of 'doing justice' to his subjects is simply to classify them on the basis of ascertained fact, dealing in qualities, without praise or blame. At the hands of the historians, then, how will Casement fare? And how will the facts recorded in *The Black Diaries* affect their estimate of his qualities?

He will remain, for the psychologist and the historian alike, an unusual example of a not unusual type—the man who, in the words of one of them, 'lives more lives than one'. We do no service to the truth, nor ('now all the truth is out') to Casement himself, by attempting to deny it or to soften it; by adopting, for instance, a recent suggestion that the 'black' entries 'read like the symptoms of a disease', that 'Casement was sick, as a drug addict is sick', and that 'he was a criminal only as an addict is, to assuage his compulsion'. It is equally false to pretend, as do the editors of *The Black Diaries*, that they record 'the anguished cry of a lonely man in each line'. It is best to face the facts: Casement, as his diaries make plain, was an insatiable invert, who enjoyed himself enormously. His tastes were all-embracing and he pursued their satisfaction with assiduity and adroitness. A great deal of his enjoyment lay in imagining and remembering, and many of the 'black' entries—mere memoranda of passing lubricities, monotonous and distasteful reading to any but the man who put them down—were evidently intended to minister to this delight in recollection.

Whether in recollection or in actuality, Casement's pleasures seem to have been entirely physical; an occasional sigh of regret—'never to meet again'—at parting from some new 'beautiful' is his nearest approach to the recording of an emotional reaction. The diaries contain no introspection, no reflection, no passion—in four short syllables: no thought, no love. If his emotions were indeed engaged during the years that are covered by this record—as they were, it seems, during his last years with the young Norwegian sailor Christensen—the diaries themselves contain no indication of the fact. One wonders what were his feelings towards the two native boys he took with him to England from the Putumayo—Omarino, 'bought' for a shirt and a pair of trousers, and Aredomi, whose 'beautiful coffee limbs' he admired so much that he tore him from a loving wife; here at least the diaries give no hint of any sexual relationship. Of course, he may have nursed unrecorded emotions and pursued lines of thought that left no shadow on his page—he did not, after all, sit down to write in the spirit of a Joubert or an Amiel; silence was prescribed by the nature of the record.

But one suspects—to judge from the sorry verses, printed in the introductory sections of *The Black Diaries*, that are all he has left to show his awareness of his own temperamental problem—that his emotions were as shallow as the intellect revealed in the clap-trap of his letters and the papers collected by Dr. Mackey. He was not to be taken seriously either as a thinker or as a lover, and his thoughts on love, if he had committed them to paper, would only have revealed the poverty of his nature; he was incapable of a *De Profundis*. And if it is shallowness of emotion that makes the 'black' pages in his diaries tedious to read, it is the lack of integrative power that makes the side of his nature that they exhibit irrelevant to the main purposes of his life; the several Casements recognized by us seem barely to have been acquainted with one another.

There, perhaps, lies the key to Casement's failure to impress himself upon us, either as a personality or as a force in the politics of rebellion: a lack of emotional depth and intellectual power, the absence of an integrated personality. He responded vividly to whatever attracted or repelled his fancy or his imagination: the thought of human cruelty in the Congo, the idea of English tyranny in his native land—to these he responded as eagerly, as obsessively, as to the human objects that stirred his physical desires; but his response was mere reaction. His fight in the Congo was a fight against Leopold rather than on behalf of his victims and, as he himself put it, 'more with [i.e. against] the Foreign Office almost than against Leopold'. And though he was capable of pity and of indignation, his lack of the deeper and more positive attributes of mind and heart was fatal to his pretensions, alike as a missionary and as a revolutionist. Great lives are not thus inspired; his efforts for his fellow-creatures seem trivial beside the story of a life like Schweitzer's, and compared with the broken eloquence of Vanzetti the rhetoric of his final plea before his judges has a hollow ring.

The Poetry of John Betjeman[1]

I n the Preface to his second collection of verses—*Old Lights for New Chancels*—John Betjeman described the kind of poetry he most enjoys; and it is the kind that the best of his own poetry belongs to. Most of the pieces in that book, and in his later volume—*New Bats in Old Belfries*—are inspired by what he calls his 'topographical predilection': they describe a scene, or convey the atmosphere of a place. If there are figures in the foreground, they are subordinate to their setting and somehow expressive of it; and even when the poem tells a story the incidents seem to be designed to make the landscape articulate, to give a voice, as it were, to the atmosphere of the Lincolnshire fens or the lakes of Westmeath or the London suburbs.

Yet, though these poems owe so much to places and their associations, they are not 'Nature poems'; though he is moved by what he sees around him, and especially by what he sees around him in the country-side, their author indulges in no reflections upon it, still less upon the feelings it evokes in him. He is content to observe, and—however deeply he may feel—to describe only what he sees and hears. In other words, he is not a Nature poet, like Wordsworth, but a landscape poet, like Crabbe. And, like Crabbe, he is the painter of the particular, the recognizable, landscape; his trees are not merely real trees with their roots in the earth, they are conifers with their roots in the red sand of Camberley, 'feathery ash in leathery Lambourne', or forsythia in the Banbury Road. For there is a great variety of landscape in his poems; unlike most pastoral poets, each of whom has his own 'especial rural scene'—Crabbe on the Suffolk coast, Cowper on the banks of the Ouse, Barnes among the farms of Dorsetshire—this poet is equally at home in the most diverse

[1] Expanded from the Preface to *Selected Poems by John Betjeman*, 1948.

surroundings—in the tame Thames valley:

> *In mud and elder-scented shade*
> *A reach away the breach is made*
>   *By dive and shout*
>   *That circles out*
> *To Henley tower and town;*
>   *And 'Boats for Hire' the rafters ring,*
>   *And pink on white the roses cling,*
>   *And red the bright geraniums swing*
>   *In baskets dangling down—*

and on the wild Cornish coast:

> *But when a storm was at its height,*
> *And feathery slate was black in rain,*
> *And tamarisks were hung with light*
> *And golden sand was brown again,*
> *Spring tide and blizzard would unite*
> *And sea came flooding up the lane—*

among the Lincolnshire fens:

> *Oh cold was the ev'ning and tall was the tower*
> *And strangely compelling the tenor bell's power!*
> *As loud on the reed-beds and strong through the dark*
> *It toll'd from the church in the tenantless park.*
>
> *The mansion was ruined, the empty demesne*
> *Was slowly reverting to marshland again—*
> *Marsh where the village was, grass in the Hall,*
> *And the Church and the Rectory waiting to fall—*

and in an Irish churchyard:

> *There in pinnacled protection,*
>   *One extinguished family waits*
> *A Church of Ireland resurrection*
>   *By the broken, rusty gates.*
> *Sheepswool, straw and droppings cover*
> *Graves of spinster, rake and lover,*

The Poetry of John Betjeman

Whose fantastic mausoleum
Sings its own sea-blown Te Deum,
In and out the slipping slates.

Plainly, what inspired the writer of those stanzas was a sense of place. Just as some people are fascinated by human beings, by their diversity and their peculiarities, so he has been fascinated by the peculiarities of various places, enjoying each simply for being what it is. Plainly, too, besides this unusual sensibility, he possesses the still rarer gift of being able to seize upon the effective features of each scene and endow them with an appropriate form and rhythm, to set them to their own peculiar tune.

This topographical predilection, as he calls it, draws him not only to the country-side, where earlier pastoral poets have sought to indulge it, but to the town and, above all, to the suburbs. For the landscape that most appeals to him is the inhabited landscape: he cannot see a place without seeing also the life that is lived in it, without becoming conscious of its human associations. Like a portrait painter, interested not so much in the beauty as in the contours of a face and in the personality that moulds it, he can find matter for poetry in the least promising surroundings, provided they have an individual character and are linked with life. So, the threat of invasion wakes in him fears for the Margate of his childhood:

> *From third floor and fourth floor the children looked down*
> *Upon ribbons of light in the salt-scented town;*
> *And drowning the trams roared the sound of the sea*
> *As it washed in the shingle the scraps of their tea.*

> *Beside the Queen's Highcliffe now rank grows the vetch,*
> *Now dark is the terrace, a storm-battered stretch;*
> *And I think, as the fairy-lit sights I recall,*
> *It is these we are fighting for, foremost of all—*

and similar echoes reach him in the purlieus of Parliament Hill Fields:

> *Oh the after-tram-ride quiet, when we heard, a mile beyond,*
> *Silver music from the bandstand, barking dogs by Highgate Pond;*

The Poetry of John Betjeman

Up the hill where stucco houses in Virginia creeper drown—
And my childish wave of pity, seeing children carrying down
Sheaves of drooping dandelions to the courts of Kentish Town.

He loves certain places—country, suburb, town—for what they have meant to him. To him they are like people; one is fond of them because they have been kind to one; one is attached to them because they belong to one's background, because they form part of one's life. Where such an attachment exists, ugliness itself can be endearing. 'I see no harm,' he writes, 'in trying to describe over-built Surrey in verse. . . . I love suburbs and gas-lights and Pont Street and Gothic Revival churches and mineral railways, provincial towns and garden cities.' Seen through his eyes—and he himself sees them through the eyes of the people who built, and the people who inhabit them—even Croydon and North Oxford exhale an unsuspected charm.

To see these things, and to reveal them to others as Mr. Betjeman has done, is to contribute something new to poetry. But this ready sensibility, this versatility of taste, may easily become a snare to its possessor. The habit of judging things simply as specimens of their kind serves, no doubt, to extend the range of one's appreciation and to refine its edge; like a sense of 'period', it opens the eyes to beauties and oddities of which others may be unaware; but, like all exploitations of taste, by tending towards concentration upon the foreground, it may obscure a wider vision. Absorbed in their appreciation of Pont Street, its victims may lose sight of the beauty of St. Paul's, and even persuade themselves, with a certain sense of triumph, that they derive a deeper pleasure from any Sandemanian Meeting-house than from Salisbury Cathedral.

In his earliest verses, collected in *Mount Zion* and *Continual Dew*, Mr. Betjeman was in danger of yielding to the seduction of the 'original' and the 'amusing'; he seemed content to lose himself in his new-found wonder-land of Victorian and post-Victorian architecture:

> *The Gothic is bursting over the way*
> *With Evangelical Song,*
> *For the pinnacled Wesley Memorial Church*
> *Is over a hundred strong,*

The Poetry of John Betjeman

And what is a new Jerusalem
Gas-lit and yellow wall'd
To a semi-circular pitchpine sea
With electric light install'd?

His sense of period, and of certain periods in particular; his eye for detail; his relish for architectural and ecclesiastical eccentricities; his delight in this newly discovered field of poetry and his facility in exploiting it—all these threatened to inhibit him from extending his range of subject or of feeling. And here his admirers were his enemies: for his early verses gained him an audience of devotees who seemed to ask only that he should continue to amuse them by further variations on the theme of his own invention:

Oh worship the Lord in the beauty of ugliness!

It looked, indeed, as if Mr. Betjeman was fated to end his days as the Laureate of the suburbs and the Gothic Revival—a position which he had, certainly, created and made his own, but one which was far from doing justice to his powers.

There is no need to dwell on the qualities which made some of his early poems so popular, any more than on their defects: the felicities and the false notes both lie obviously on the surface. The lines on the arrest of Oscar Wilde are an attempt to create an atmosphere of 'period' by wheeling the old stage-properties—the astrakhan coat, the hock and the seltzer, *The Yellow Book*—all too conscientiously into place; while as for *Death in Leamington*, that is Mr. Betjeman's *Innisfree*, doomed to haunt its author, in too persistent popularity, all his days.

The peculiarity of his best work, however, results from an eccentricity that is quite unaffected and a sophistication that is entirely natural. It is when he looks at life from his own odd angles that his poetry is most successful. He really sees a poem in such situations as 'Sudden Illness at the Bus Stop', 'Invasion Exercise on the Poultry Farm', 'The Irish Unionist's Farewell to Greta Hellstrom in 1922'. And who but he would find poetry—mingled with reminiscences of Yeats and Francis Thompson—in the licorice fields of the West Riding?

The Poetry of John Betjeman

In the licorice fields at Pontefract
My love and I did meet
And many a burdened licorice bush
Was blooming round our feet;
Red hair she had and golden skin,
Her sulky lips were shaped for sin,
Her sturdy legs were flannel-slack'd,
The strongest legs in Pontefract. . . .

She cast her blazing eyes on me
And plucked a licorice leaf:
I was her captive slave and she
My red-haired robber chief.
Oh love! for love I could not speak;
It left me winded, wilting, weak
And held in brown arms strong and bare
And wound with flaming ropes of hair.

Nothing could well be stranger or more sophisticated than that. To call it 'amusing' would be an inadequate, if not an inaccurate, description: it is at once a successful picture and a successful poem. When he chooses a more conventionally emotional situation, Mr. Betjeman seems to make a poem out of it rather than to see a poem in it, and the result is not so happy. Witness the brave little wife on the specialist's doorstep in 'Devonshire Street, W.1':

> *No hope. And the X-ray photographs under his arm*
> *Confirm the message. His wife stands timidly by—*

and the dying night-club proprietress in 'Sun and Fun':

> *But I'm dying now and done for.*
> *What on earth was all the fun for?—*

the touch has faltered, the thing does not come off.

Equally—and this perhaps is more surprising—the touch falters, the materials do not fuse, in those poems which seem to be direct expressions of personal emotion, such as 'Remorse', 'Portrait of a

[171]

Deaf Man', 'Pershore Station', and 'A Child Ill':

> *So looked my father at the last*
> *Right in my soul, before he died.*
> *Though words we spoke went heedless past*
> *As London traffic-roar outside.*

> *And now the same blue eyes I see*
> *Look through me from a little son,*
> *So questioning, so searchingly*
> *That youthfulness and age are one.*

One does not doubt the sincerity or the depth of the feeling, any more than one doubts the depth and sincerity of the feeling that inspires his diatribes on the Hygienic Public House, Welfare Cities in a Welfare State, and the inanities of 'Progressive' talks on Sex in the Civic Centre; but somehow neither in elegy nor in satire does the feeling fuse into poetry. It seems that Mr. Betjeman's subject must reach him from a distance, along the paths of imagination or of memory, if it is to 'inspire' him. Then he can give us poems of fantasy and description which lift him out of the ranks of 'minor' poets. For fantasy, take 'Sir John Piers' or 'The Heart of Thomas Hardy', a Stanley Spencer vision of resurrection in a country churchyard; for imaginative description, take the closing lines of 'Beside the Seaside':

> *And all the time the waves, the waves, the waves*
> *Chase, intersect and flatten on the sand*
> *As they have done for centuries, as they will*
> *For centuries to come, when not a soul*
> *Is left to picnic on the blazing rocks,*
> *When England is not England, when mankind*
> *Has blown himself to pieces. Still the sea,*
> *Consolingly disastrous, will return*
> *While the strange starfish, hugely magnified,*
> *Waits in the jewelled basin of a pool—*

and for reminiscent description, the following miraculous passage

The Poetry of John Betjeman

from 'North Coast Recollections';

> *So on this after-storm-lit evening*
> *To Jim the raindrops in the tamarisk,*
> *The fuchsia bells, the sodden matchbox lid*
> *That checked a tiny torrent in the lane,*
> *Were magnified and shining clear with life.*
> *Then pealing out across the estuary*
> *The Padstow bells rang up for practice-night*
> *An undersong to birds and dripping shrubs.*
> *The full Atlantic at September spring*
> *Flooded a final tide-mark up the sand,*
> *And ocean sank to silence under bells,*
> *And the next breaker was a lesser one*
> *Then lesser still. Atlantic, bells and birds*
> *Were layer on interchanging layer of sound.*

The second part of *Old Lights for New Chancels* consists of poems which their author calls 'amatory'. Perhaps this name will serve for them as well as any other; to call them love-poems would be as misleading as to call his topographical verses nature-poetry, and misleading in the same direction. Between these two kinds of poems there is a curious analogy: fascinated by certain features of the human landscape, he describes Miss Joan Hunter Dunn as though she were a part of Surrey—lingering upon its surface, surrendering to its associations, and making his picture of it live by his unerring choice of detail. He does not analyse his feeling for his tennis-partner any more than he analyses his feeling for the Coulsdon woodlands; we have to gauge its depth simply from the warmth of his description. How deep, how 'serious', that emotion may be it is difficult to say, and perhaps foolish to ask. But at least it is clear that, when his eyes are turned towards the landscape of sex, Mr. Betjeman's vision does not range beyond the features that can be seen from the foothills of childhood and adolescence; not for him the scent and the sympathy, the soulful or the sophisticated allurements, of mature femininity; he revives the passions of the school holidays, of the birthday party and the tennis tournament—emotions that were devastating out of all proportion to their depth, simply because they were too strong and

[173]

full for the channels along which they were forced to flow:

> *First love, first light, first life. A heartbeat noise!*
> *His heart or little feet? A snap of twigs*
> *Dry, dead and brown the under-branches part*
> *And Bonzo scrambles by their secret way.*
> *First love so deep, John Lambourn cannot speak,*
> *So deep, he feels a tightening in his throat,*
> *So tender, he could brush away the sand*
> *Dried up in patches on her freckled legs,*
> *Could hold her gently till the stars went down,*
> *And if she cut herself would staunch the wound,*
> *Yes, even with his First Eleven scarf,*
> *And hold it there for hours.*

If he were a novelist, Mr. Betjeman would be the novelist of child-hood: he remembers so well what it was like to be a child, and how the world looked through the sharp eyes of one who was still seeing things close to, and for the first time:

> *Oh when the early morning at the seaside*
> *Took us with hurrying steps from Horsey Mere*
> *To see the whistling bent-grass on the leeside*
> *And then the tumbled breaker-line appear,*
> *On high, the clouds with mighty adumbration*
> *Sailed over us to seaward fast and clear*
> *And jelly-fish in quivering isolation*
> *Lay silted in the dry sand of the breeze*
> *And we, along the table-land of beach blown*
> *Went gooseflesh from our shoulders to our knees*
> *And ran to catch the football, each to each thrown,*
> *In the soft and swirling music of the seas.*

The sea, and the days of his childhood—these are the sources from which spring almost all the most deeply felt (and they are also the most deeply moving) of his poems, and when those sources are united, as they are in his poems about Cornwall, the force of his creative emotion is at its strongest.

Other impulses move him to write, among them a bent for satire,

or something very like it. *In a Bath Teashop* might be a sketch by
Thomas Hardy, and *The Planster's Vision* reveals his loathing of the
socialized world into which he has had the misfortune to be born:

> *Cut down that timber! Bells too many and strong*
> *Pouring their music through the branches bare*
> *From moon-white church-towers down the windy air*
> *Have pealed the centuries out with Evensong.*
> *Remove those cottages, a huddled throng!*
> *Too many babies have been born in there,*
> *Too many coffins, bumping down the stair,*
> *Carried the old their garden paths along . . .*

But satire is not his *forte*: despite the moving lines just quoted, the
sestet of the sonnet from which they are taken, and such early poems
as *Slough* and *In Westminster Abbey*, hardly rise above the level of the
political lampoons in a weekly magazine. He possesses all the gifts
that make a satirist except the gift of indignation. He has an eye for
the external peculiarities of his fellow-creatures, and insight into the
qualities that go with them. Put him in the hall of the Regent Palace
Hotel or on the seafront at Blackpool or in the bar of a Bloomsbury
public-house, and he will tell you all about the tastes and habits of
those around him—the businessmen with portly stomachs and the
intellectuals with pasty faces, the young men who sell motor-cars
and the girls they go about with: no facet of their ugliness or vulgarity escapes him. But so completely is he fascinated by what he
sees, so absorbed by curiosity about his fellow-beings, that he quite
forgets his natural distaste. Instinctively, he is interested in them
and 'amused' by them, as he is interested and amused by specimens
of architecture; they are, after all, also the works of a creator. Each
individual is to him, quite literally, a specimen of humanity, and his
feeling for humanity is such that figures which others might find
merely unattractive seem to him pathetic, and where a satirist would
feel indignation or disgust he feels compassion. It is compassion that
is stirred in him, for instance, as he gazes on a crowd of Christmas
shoppers:

> *And girls in slacks remember Dad*
> *And oafish louts remember Mum*

[175]

The Poetry of John Betjeman

And sleeping children's hearts are glad
And Christmas morning bells say 'Come!'
Even to the shining ones who dwell
Safe in the Dorchester Hotel.

That is not satire: if you are to satirize human beings you must be angry with them, not sorry for them; you must look at them uncompromisingly from outside, refusing all temptations to see the world through their eyes or them through the eyes of their creator—in other words you must divest yourself of that imaginative sympathy which is Mr. Betjeman's distinctive gift as a poet, whether he is writing about places, or buildings, or human beings.

Mr. Betjeman is much obsessed with the fear of death, and spares us none of its horrors.

> *Oh why* [he asks] *do people waste their breath*
> *Inventing dainty names for death?*—

and this fear, in *Before the Anaesthetic*, inspires him to write a really remarkable and terrifying poem. Here again, childhood reminiscence plays its part; his fear is still the fear that he caught from the 'cheap nursery maid' he tells us of in one of his poems, and for more than one of his most poignant lyrics he might have borrowed Alice Meynell's title, 'Intimations of Mortality, from Recollections of Early Childhood'.

His 'religious' poetry springs from the same source. Almost all of it, like 'Sunday Afternoon Service in St. Enodoc Church, Cornwall', draws upon the recollection of going to church as a child. 'Almost all,' for in one or two pieces—and here his touch is as uncertain as it is in elegy and in satire—he seeks to convey the mystical adoration with which he reveres the sacrament of the Mass; the rest of his 'religious' poetry is not religious poetry but Church poetry—Church of England poetry:

> *'I acknowledge my transgressions'*
> *The well-known phrases rolled*
> *With thunder sailing over*
> *From the heavily clouded wold.*
> *'And my sin is ever before me'*

[176]

The Poetry of John Betjeman

> *There in the lighted East*
> *He stood in that lowering sunlight,*
> *An Indian Christian priest.*

Has the very note of the English Church ever been so surely seized and so clearly reproduced? Only by one earlier poet:

> *We have done with dogma and divinity.*
> *Easter and Whitsun past,*
> *The long, long Sundays after Trinity*
> *Are with us at last;*
> *The passionless Sundays after Trinity,*
> *Neither feast-day nor fast. . . .*

> *Post pugnam pausa fiet:*
> *Lord, we have made our choice;*
> *In the stillness of autumn quiet,*
> *We have heard the still, small voice.*
> *We have sung* Oh where shall Wisdom?
> *Thick paper, folio, Boyce.*

Could anything be purer Betjeman than those stanzas? Well, perhaps the following:

> *On the fly-leaves of these old prayer-books*
> *The childish writings fade,*
> *Which show that once they were their books*
> *In the days when prayer was made*
> *For other Kings and princesses,*
> *William and Adelaide.*

> *The pillars are twisted with holly,*
> *And the font is wreathed with yew;*
> *Christ forgive me for folly,*
> *Youth's lapses—not a few,*
> *For the hardness of my middle life,*
> *For age's fretful view.*

There is no need to suppose that Mr. Betjeman ever saw the privately printed little book of Mead Falkner's verses from which these are taken. Even if he was familiar with it, the resemblance may be accounted for simply by affinity—the Church of England note echoing with identical cadences and rhyme-tricks, in two kindred and receptive consciousnesses.

The Church of England note sounds with a different cadence in his little-known collection *Poems in the Porch*. Introducing those delightful verses, their author modestly said that 'they do not pretend to be poetry'. But whether or not all Mr. Betjeman's verse is poetry, all his poetry is verse, and in this it is a pleasant change from the shapeless and unarticulated matter, the 'fluid puddings', offered us by so many of his contemporaries. He delights the ear by the sound of his words, the run of his lines, the shape of his stanzas.

Not that his metres are recondite, or worked out in accordance with any theory: he trusts, evidently, to his ear and to his natural exuberance, and reproduces with his own *ex tempore* elaborations echoes of things that have caught his fancy in Father Prout or Praed or Dibdin or Tom Moore. Sometimes our pleasure in reading him springs from these auditory associations, from hearing, as it were, a new song set to an old tune; sometimes the tune and pattern are his own, as in *Wantage Bells*:

> *Wallflowers are bright in their beds*
> *   And their scent all pervading,*
> *Withered are primroses' heads*
> *   And the hyacinth fading,*
> *But flowers by the score*
> *Multitudes more*
> *Weed flowers and seed flowers and mead flowers*
> *   our paths are invading.*
>
> *Where are the words to express*
> *   Such a reckless bestowing?*
> *The voices of birds utter less*
> *   Than the thanks we are owing.*
> *Bell notes alone*
> *Ring praise of their own*
> *As clear as the weed-waving brook*
> *   and as evenly flowing.*

The Poetry of John Betjeman

'Where are the words?' Mr. Betjeman has found them; they solicit the ear with an artistry almost as sure and as subtle as Tennyson's.[1] And it is not caprice, nor merely the desire for euphony, that dictates the highly original conformation of many of his stanzas, but an instinctive sense of tune, of the way in which the shape of a stanza can help in the expression of what the poet has to say; and it is this sense, quite as much as his idiosyncrasy of vision and of feeling, that makes him a unique figure among contemporary poets.

[1] I say 'almost' for he is a careless and far from faultless metrist. In the second of the two stanzas quoted above, the third line would probably, and the last line certainly, be improved by the removal of its first syllable.

A Difficult Topic[1]

'Is it true,' asked Lord Winterton recently in the House of Lords, 'that homosexuals, being admittedly peculiar and in many cases vain creatures, glory in the prison sentence as a form of advertisement?' There is certainly no trace of any such peculiar vanity in Mr. Wildeblood's book. His account of what he suffered in prison, and outside it, makes it clear that publicity was one of the most painful elements in his punishment, and it might have been with such a case as his in mind that A. E. Housman wrote his bitterly satirical tirade about the 'young sinner with the handcuffs on his wrists':

> Oh a deal of pains he's taken and a pretty price he's paid
> To hide his poll or dye it of a mentionable shade;
> But they've pulled the beggar's hat off for the world to see and stare,
> And they're haling him to justice for the colour of his hair.

Lord Winterton's question was not, of course, intended to imply any tenderness on his part towards what he calls a 'filthy, unnatural, and disgusting vice', and an interesting appendix to the second of the two books before us quotes some fiery diatribes delivered by him and by Lord Vansittart in a recent debate held in the House of Lords on this perplexing topic—a topic on which Lord Samuel also has made some eloquent contributions in the same spirit.

A perplexing topic—and none the less perplexing because it provokes extreme expressions of feeling and opinion on either side. To the extremists of each party their case seems so clear as hardly to admit of opposition. Rant on the one part about 'this filthy vice' is

[1] A review of *Against the Law* by Peter Wildeblood and *They Stand Apart*, edited by J. Tudor Rees and H. V. Usill, 1955.

[180]

matched on the other by an equally determined refusal to see in the law that condemns it anything but an antiquated anomaly upheld by 'stupid prejudice'. Between these extremes are ranged a number of serious-minded people, to most of whom the subject is familiar only through reports of proceedings in the Courts and in Parliament, who know that religion, morality, and psychology all lay claim to have their say upon it, and who would find it difficult, if asked their own opinion, to decide what that opinion really is. Both the books before us, if they do not enable such inquirers to make up their minds upon the problem, will at least give them a fuller view of it.

Of the two, Mr. Wildeblood's will no doubt be the more widely read, for it has the appeal of a 'human document'. In the words of its publishers, it is the inside story of a *cause célèbre*, told by one of its 'central figures', who has used all the talents of a 'skilled journalist' to enhance its sentimental appeal. It is sincere in intention and at certain points it is a moving story. In particular, Mr. Wildeblood's description of his experience in prison, though it is marred by mawkishness, and though he finds it easier to criticize short-comings in the prison system than to suggest practicable methods of improving it, rises at times above the level of lively reporting which is evidently his *métier*.

As an account of trial and imprisonment and of their effect upon the writer's attitude to life, *Against the Law* calls irresistibly for comparison with Wilde's *De Profundis*. Like Wilde, Mr. Wildeblood saw that prison and the experiences leading up to it must be mastered and digested; that something must, as it were, be made of them; that it was his task to rise above bitterness against others and pity for himself. In Wilde's nature there was a deep spring of generosity which helped him to achieve this: after his release he never sought to deny his guilt; he never railed against the prosecution (though Queensberry and Carson had been implacable and savage in their pursuit); he was never vindictive towards those who gave evidence against him; and his treatment of the friend whose vanity and selfishness were the immediate cause of his downfall was remarkable for its magnanimity. These attributes of its author lend to *De Profundis*, in spite of its passages of shallow and sentimental philosophizing, a nobility that is entirely absent from Mr. Wildeblood's *apologia*. It is not merely that Wilde was an artist and Mr. Wildeblood is a journalist; the difference lies in the personalities of the two men; Wilde, for all his self-dramatization, may claim to be considered a martyr, whatever one may think of the cause in which he suffered; Mr. Wildeblood is a man with a grievance, or with a string of grievances. He has not succeeded in the effort to keep out of his book all bitterness except 'the bitterness of medicine'; there is bitterness, of a different sort, at every stage: bitterness about 'the rigidity of the English class system', bitterness about 'the men at the top' in his own profession ('a cold-eyed bunch of business men who peddled tragedy'), bitterness about lawyers ('At the end of a long career at the Bar they must have become like stones, washed clean of . . . all regard for truth—and it was then, by a singular stroke of irony, that they were made into judges'), bitterness about the House of Lords (he scoffs at the hearing-aid of one 'noble lord', the 'beautiful suit' of another) bitterness (how unlike Wilde!) against the wretched youth whose evidence was his undoing (defending counsel, he says, 'looked at McNally as though he were something sticking to a spade'; 'it seemed incredible that I could have written such words to such a man'). It is easy to understand that attitude in one who has undergone, before and after conviction, the experiences described by Mr. Wildeblood; but it detracts both from the dignity of his book and from the effectiveness of its plea. It leads him to cast (no doubt in all good faith) wild aspersions upon men who are precluded, by their positions, from replying to them. And it leads him to harp upon alleged irregularities in the proceedings taken against him which, even if admitted, are irrelevant to the main case that he sets out to plead—the case of the homosexual offender who has had not an unfair deal at the hands of the law, but a fair one.

At one point Mr. Wildeblood goes significantly wrong: he suggests that a jury which acquits on one charge, thus demonstrating its mistrust of vital witnesses for the prosecution, is guilty of inconsistency if it does not acquit on other charges for which their evidence is equally important. Perhaps it is. But jurors often believe such witnesses to be fundamentally truthful, and having no doubt about a prisoner's guilt on one charge, yet feel that there is enough doubt about their evidence on another charge to enable them to say that guilt has not been fully proved. If that is inconsistent it is an inconsistency for which many a prisoner has had reason to be grateful.

Perhaps the most unfortunate defect in Mr. Wildeblood's book is an ambiguity that lies at its very centre: he recounts at length his trial and the events that led up to it without at any point asserting that he was innocent of all that was charged against him or admitting that he was not. This leaves an uncomfortable sense of prevarication; Mr. Wildeblood has undertaken to write his book in the hope of helping those who are justly, not those who are unjustly, charged with such offences; he has himself, as he says at the outset, 'nothing left to hide'; and his book suffers, both as a plea for others and as a psychological study, from his failure to be explicit, one way or the other, upon this central question.

Mr. Wildeblood's book, with all its defects, stands as a personal plea that the law should allow the homosexual to 'live his own life'. That plea raises issues which are not as simple as Mr. Wildeblood evidently supposes. The second book before us sets out to give a balanced survey of the problem. It is a problem on which people's opinions will be influenced, if not determined, by their religious beliefs and by their views of the moral principles or rules of social expediency which should govern conduct; and in applying such rules and principles to it they will wish to take into account medical and scientific evidence. So *They Stand Apart* contains sections on Christian Morals, Society, and the Law, and also an extended examination of 'The Medical Aspects'.

The most interesting and the most closely argued contribution to the symposium is Dr. D. S. Bailey's examination of the question from a Christian's point of view. Dr. Bailey describes the origins and development of the Christian attitude and attempts to determine what should be the present-day Christian's answer to the questions 'Are homosexual acts intrinsically sinful? How far and in what circumstances are they blameworthy? Should they be criminally punishable?' In a brief historical survey he glances at the influences —the Old and New Testaments, the Penitentials, the Roman law, the Rationalists' conception of 'nature', the 'nexus of socio-psychological factors underlying and determining to no small degree the sexual ideas of a community, an age, or a culture'—that have shaped the Western Christian tradition, and states the 'ineluctable conclusion' reached by that tradition as follows:

'The use of the sexual organs, being governed by the nature of sex itself and by recognized purposes of coitus, is proper only in the context of a personal relation which is both heterosexual and specifically marital. Considered, then, in terms of objective morality, it is evident that homosexual acts are contrary to the will of God for human sexuality, and are therefore sinful *per se.*'

It is not clear what is meant here by the key phrase 'being governed by' or by the words that immediately follow it; but if one accepts Dr. Bailey's conception of 'the will of God for human sexuality' one must admit his conclusion that though homosexual love can be an elevated emotion the moral law forbids its expression in sexual acts—'a limitation', he adds, 'which it shares with all forms of heterosexual relationship but one'—namely, the relationship of marriage.

Dr. Bailey points out that not all intrinsically sinful acts render the agent morally blameworthy, and he inquires into the culpability of those who in various circumstances commit this particular sin. Such acts, he says, are almost invariably free, the only exceptions being the rare cases where the agent suffers from such a severe psychopathic condition that his acts are no more free than are those of (say) the kleptomaniac. Indeed, the defence of 'irresistible impulse' receives short shrift in this book from moralist, lawyer, and doctor alike: the patient may not be able to help being what he is, but, in ninety-nine cases out of a hundred, he can help doing what he does. The degree of culpability of the agent in regard to any particular free act, however, will vary in accordance with whether he acts in 'vincible' or 'invincible' ignorance of its moral quality; each case will require individual determination by the casuist.

Finally, Dr. Bailey discusses the criminal aspect of the subject. Crime, as he says, does not necessarily imply moral wrongdoing, and sin is not and cannot be always punishable by the State. It is not the purpose of the law to safeguard private morality, and it would be neither practicable nor right to punish fornication or adultery with criminal sanctions. Dr. Bailey sees no ground—either in the nature of the act or in its social consequences—for treating homosexuality differently in this respect from other sexual immorality:

'The present legal proscription of homosexuality [he concludes] is thus an anachronism, and its conspicuous lack of success is sufficient proof that this method of trying to enforce moral behaviour upon the subject is futile. . . . The private sexual sins of the individual . . . are moral offences for which he or she must normally be held culpable; yet at the same time they are regarded as acts of wrong doing which, by reason of their peculiar character, cannot properly be prevented or punished by the State. And from this category of immoral sexual acts which are deemed not to be cognizable by the law there would seem to be no justification for excluding male homosexual practices.'

He would, however, retain such provisions as are necessary in order to safeguard young persons and to preserve public decency.

Dr. Bailey's view of the moral quality of acts of the kind under discussion follows from his religious beliefs: such acts are wrong because they are 'contrary to the will of God for human sexuality'. Lord Hailsham, who contributes to this symposium an interesting discussion of 'Homosexuality and Society', accepts Dr. Bailey's religious premise: 'The moral question involved in homosexuality,' he says, 'is not one which anyone accepting the Jewish or Christian moral tradition can possibly accept as open.' But he realizes that it is necessary to address himself to those who do not accept the religious assumption because they cannot attach a meaning to the phrase 'the will of God for human sexuality'. He therefore proceeds to discuss the moral and social aspects of the problem, leaving religion out of account.

His conclusion is that these practices are both immoral and antisocial, and that their consequences must be so deleterious to society as to warrant the application of criminal sanctions to prevent them. He does not reach this conclusion without much reflection, and a natural reluctance to extend the interference of the criminal law in the sphere of private actions.

A Difficult Topic

On the way to his conclusion, Lord Hailsham rightly distinguishes between inclination or affection and overt acts. A repressed sexual affection for members of one's own sex (he says) may inspire a saintly and dedicated life: the law would not condemn such an 'inclination' nor (he suggests) would morality. But if it issues in overt acts, those acts, he feels, merit condemnation on moral grounds, and they should certainly be prohibited by law.

His argument runs as follows: the popular instinct to call such acts 'unnatural' (in a sense in which fornication and adultery are not unnatural) is a sound one; they are not necessarily therefore immoral (for 'many unnatural acts are . . . morally indifferent'); they are immoral because they involve a misuse of non-complementary physical organs which almost inevitably has deplorable psycholological consequences for the parties concerned, and because a relationship with such an unsatisfactory physical basis can rarely if ever be a lasting physical or spiritual relationship; further, 'its necessarily sterile outcome from the point of view of the procreation of children also deprives it of the basis of lasting comradeship which in natural parenthood often succeeds the passionate romance of earlier days'. (The keyword in the foregoing passage appears to be the word 'misuse', which Lord Hailsham would justify partly by reference to physical conformation—the argument from design—and partly by an appeal to physical and psychological effects; his strictures closely correspond with Dr. Bailey's thesis that the organization of the human body is such that a homosexual 'union' cannot achieve satisfactorily the 'relational', or achieve at all the 'conceptual', ends which a Christian must feel to be the proper ends of love.)

Much of this is indisputable: such relationships are 'unnatural' in the ordinary sense of the word; they can rarely if ever be fully 'satisfactory', and they can never achieve the complete fulfilment which can be found in heterosexual love, and especially in married life. That is the misfortune of the homosexual, who is often no doubt a less harmonious and efficient, as well as a less happy, member of society because he is what he is. It is not equally clear that he is therefore to be condemned on moral as distinct from social grounds.

[186]

The purely ethical question, however, is irrelevant to Lord Hailsham's conclusion; for him the determining factor is the social danger which (he says) arises because such people are always 'proselytisers' and seek their converts among the young, who are peculiarly liable to become 'fixed' in the habits into which they are initiated and so become proselytisers in their turn. Thus there is developed 'a self-perpetuating and potentially widely expansible secret society of addicts to a practice ultimately harmful to the adjustment of the individual to his surroundings and effecting a permanent and detrimental change in his personality'. Unless this process is checked by law, Lord Hailsham foresees 'a degree of corruption quite beyond the experience of any contemporary civilized society of Christian origins'.

Some of the links in the chain of argument that leads to this alarming conclusion are certainly confirmed by the specialist evidence, which shows that assaults on the young may 'start a conditioning process' that awakens latent homosexual tendencies, which are far more widely distributed in youth than is generally supposed, and which, once awakened, may persist into manhood. The danger to youth, however, and the consequent danger to society at large, could be met, one would have thought, by retaining so far as concerns young persons the present provisions of the law, as Dr. Bailey would propose. Lord Hailsham's answer on this point is not convincing: 'If homosexuality is in truth something which is socially so dangerous that it is to be prohibited before the age of twenty-one, I should have thought,' he says, 'that the balance of advantage lay in prohibiting it altogether.' If we ask why the same argument should not apply in the case of heterosexual offences, no doubt Lord Hailsham's answer would be that, quite apart from the impracticability of treating fornication as a crime, it is not such a serious social danger as are the practices he seeks to prohibit. But he lays so much stress in his argument upon the corruption of youth as the avenue of danger to society that it is difficult to see why he should feel that the balance of advantage is against a proposal which, while respecting the principle that the law does not interfere in the sphere of private morality, checks at its very source the danger against which he desires to guard.

A Difficult Topic

Even less cogent is the objection which Lord Hailsham regards as 'most important and possibly even conclusive'. The existence of homosexuality, he says, in schools and sporting and military organizations engenders 'jealousies and favouritisms' which 'undermine and disintegrate the whole fabric of social co-operation', and its existence in a profession, if widespread, renders that profession 'less attractive, if not intolerable, to normal people'. It is a commonplace that the undetermined sexual inclinations of adolescence provide schools with one of their most difficult problems; but it is difficult to see how that problem would be aggravated by a change in the law which affected only relations between adults, or to believe that such a change would have the alarming effect upon professional life in England that Lord Hailsham envisages.

Lord Hailsham's lurid picture of social disintegration recalls the apprehensions of the Emperor Justinian, who legislated against homosexual practices (so Dr. Bailey tells us) in the belief that they were directly or indirectly the cause of earthquakes. That belief is doubtless no longer entertained even by Lord Samuel, but something like it must surely inspire, unconsciously, those who attack homosexuality on the ground that it is a serious danger to society. In a primitive and isolated community the practice might be dangerous if it became predominant—not as inducing degeneracy (for it has thriven not only, as Dante says, among *letterati grandi* but in virile and military societies such as Sparta and modern Germany) but because it might be a threat to the reproductiveness of the race. In the modern world, and in present circumstances, that threat is surely something of a bogy.

Why, then, are such misconceived attacks delivered with so much sincerity and such force? Because, we suggest, they are rationalizations of a feeling which is left out of account by Dr. Bailey and Lord Hailsham—a deep instinctive horror of the practice. This feeling has not prevailed always and everywhere (not, for instance, in Eastern countries or in ancient Greece), and there are signs that it is diminishing today in this country; but it is still powerful and widespread; it is felt by many even of those who, on principle, advocate toleration in the matter; it is felt (according to the evidence in the books before us) among homosexuals themselves. No fair-minded inquirer ought to disregard it.

How far, one must ask, is this deep-seated and widespread human instinct based on reason? If it is irrational, what is its cause? And how far, in either alternative, should it be taken into account by the legislator?

The most obvious explanation is that it is a horror of the unnatural. Philosophers give short shrift to the conception of 'the natural' once it is deprived of a religious basis; it implies, they say, a design without a designer, and is therefore meaningless. We may well prefer to recognize the force of common speech, if not of common sense, and allow the 'unnaturalness' of homosexual practices; but even so we have to admit that so much of civilized conduct runs counter to what is natural that it remains a question why this particular defiance of nature should rouse such passionate repugnance. The key lies surely in its abnormality; the herd is always ready to turn and rend the *lusus naturæ* or the freak, and the special repugnance felt for this particular form of abnormality is due to the fact that it is an abnormality of sex. Sex has always inspired a twofold *pudor*, it is both sacred and disgusting, its organs are *pudenda*—in the words of Yeats,

> *Love has pitched his mansion in*
> *The place of excrement.*

The Book of Genesis shows how deep the shame of sex is seated in the human race; men may be reconciled to its normal manifestations by knowing that they are universal and necessary for the reproduction of the race, by the very fact, also, that they minister to their own strong urges and are exalted and transmuted for them by association with their experience of the passion of love. But when sex manifests itself in an abnormal form and with none of these accompaniments, it receives the full force of man's natural shame and repugnance.

The strength and vitality of that repugnance are attested by the traditional language of the Statute-book ('un trop horrible vice q^u ne fait pas à nomer'; 'the abominable crime'), by such writers as the civilized and rational Gibbon ('a more odious vice, of which modesty rejects the name, and nature abominates the idea'), and by such savage outbursts as were referred to in the opening lines of this review, echoes of which may be heard in the smoking room of any club and in many a barrack room and bar parlour. It is on this strong repugnance, and not on any calculation of its social harmfulness, that the case for the legal prohibition of homosexuality really rests. An analogy is presented by the case of cruelty to animals, which evokes in this country today (but has not always done so, and does not in all other countries) a repugnance far greater than does cruelty to children—though the latter is obviously productive of much more damage to society. So, too, the crime of bestiality, though it cannot be said to constitute so grave a threat to society as homosexuality, evokes an even stronger disapproval in the popular mind simply because it is the more flagrant sexual abnormality: that disapproval is founded (like the disapproval of homosexuality itself) on instinctive repugnance, and not on moral or social sense.

How strong and how widespread is this repugnance in England today and how far should the legislator give effect to it in the provisions of the criminal law? These are the fundamental questions to which the members of the Commission who are now examining this subject must address themselves. As the analyses given above will have made plain, they will find little that helps them to answer it either in Mr. Wildeblood's book or in the sections of *They Stand Apart* on Christian Morals and on Society, nor will they find any more in the sections dealing with 'The Medical Aspects' and with the legal position in other countries.

Dr. Lindesay Neustatter, who is responsible for the medical section, frankly admits that neither the doctor nor the psychologist knows either the cause of the homosexual condition or any panacea for it. He discusses the various kinds of factor that have been suggested—endocrine, psychological, constitutional, and genetic—and is forced to conclude that none of the explanations is entirely satisfactory, and that none of them accounts fully for the condition. Kallmann's interesting inquiries into identical twins suggest that a constitutional factor is the cause, and it may be possible, says Dr. Neustatter, 'to analyse and resolve the so-called constitutional factors; they may for example really be an expression of some physiological dysfunction which as yet we do not understand. If so [he adds] at present there is nothing that we can do about them.'

Hence psychological theories are more popular, as opening up possibilities of a cure, but Dr. Neustatter finds it 'hard to see that any of the psychological explanations can adequately explain the more constitutional cases, and none of the psychological theories answers the question why experiences, common to all children and adults, only affect some'.

The remedies suggested in the chapter on 'Prevention and Treatment' make plain the inability of medicine or psychology or social hygiene to deal satisfactorily with this problem. 'Radical' treatment, which aims at curing the condition, either by psychotherapy or by administering hormones, has little prospect of success; and little more can be hoped from 'palliative' measures, which are designed 'to prevent the occurrence of overt sexual behaviour', either by 're-education and persuasion' or by anatomical castration or the administration of hormones which reduce the intensity but do not alter the direction of the sexual impulse. As for the convicted offender, while all seem agreed that an ordinary prison is unlikely to alter his nature, the bankruptcy of science and penology is vividly illustrated by the various alternatives suggested—confinement in lunatic asylums (or 'mental institutions'), or in prisons specially organized for sexual or homosexual offenders (which Dr. Neustatter admits to be what he quaintly calls 'a utopian dream') or in prisons where they can mix with 'feminine company'—presumably women convicts (surely a utopian nightmare?); together with such hopeful ancillary measures as the encouragement of 'after-care' by the Church and 'other organizations' and the posting in public lavatories of notices advertising 'neurosis centres'. Such suggestions will hardly help the Commission to make any very practical recommendations in the matter.

Nor is much assistance to be gleaned from Dr. Hammelmann's account of the legal position in other countries. It illustrates the diversity of treatment prevailing under various systems of law (no mention is made of Russia, where homosexual offences are, or were till recently, punishable by death), and affords material for the refutation of hasty generalizations; but it is rather interesting than positively helpful.

[191]

A Difficult Topic

We have said that the task before the Commission is difficult, and we are tempted to add that it is hopeless.

> How small, of all that human hearts endure,
> That part which laws or kings can cause or cure!

Even if the Commission, having considered the problem in its moral and its social aspects, and given as much weight as they think right to popular feeling, decide to recommend a change in the law, and legislation follows, the effect may not be so immediate or so deep as the reformers like to think:

> poena potest tolli, culpa perennis erit.

Law in such a matter does not make or govern opinion; the age-old repugnance will persist; the social stigma will be undiminished; the power of the blackmailer (whose usual threat is exposure not to the police, but to the family or the employer) will be almost as great as ever; the homosexual will be a no less lonely and frustrated figure; and his love will still be a love that dares not speak its name.

The Censor as Aedile[1]

'Limits of Control'—*The Times Literary Supplement* has recently conducted an investigation into the unseen social forces that exert their subtle pressures on a writer and determine the scope and shape of his work. Besides these hidden persuaders there exists another factor, working, so to say, on the surface, and inhibiting the writer in a practical, though not always predictable, fashion: the force of the Law.

In this country the law can hardly be said to threaten a serious encroachment upon the liberty of the writer and the reader; none the less, as Sir Charles Snow has reminded us, we ought not to allow our insularity to blind us to the fact that things are very different abroad; in the Soviet lands, for instance, Pasternak's novel is still on the Index and the citizen has recently been given a sharp reminder that it is for his masters to determine what he shall write and what he shall read. Even in Great Britain the interest displayed in the passing of the Obscene Publications Act, 1959 (the 'Jenkins Act'), and in the first test case to arise under it, has shown how strong are the feelings aroused both in writers and in the general public by our own modest efforts at state interference. Now that that stir has subsided, the publication, in summary, of the proceedings in the 'Lady Chatterley' trial and the magisterial Rede Lecture on 'Censors' recently delivered by Lord Radcliffe throw a vivid light, from different levels, on this vexed problem.

The question that underlies the whole difficult business is, of course, a fundamental one: what considerations should determine

---

[1] A review of *Regina v. Penguin Books Limited, The Transcript of the Trial*, edited by C. H. Rolph and *Censorship*, the Rede Lecture, by Lord Radcliffe, 1961.

the limits of state interference with the liberty of the individual? The activities of the censor prompt us to ask, more particularly, whether special considerations apply in the case of the spoken or written word, and whether 'literature' has any claim to exceptional treatment.

Even the most extreme libertarian will hardly deny that the censor's interference is sometimes justified. When the state is in danger, for instance, he acts as one of the security services; it is as reasonable that the law should forbid the publication of the pamphlet inciting to mutiny as it is that it should forbid the planting of the assassin's bomb. What, then, about the life and limb of the individual citizen? If the law may intervene to protect the child from cruelty and the adult from the physical attack of the bully or the more insidious assault of the drug-peddler, why (it may be asked) may it not equally intervene to protect the child—or the adult, for the matter of that— from damage inflicted by the horror film or by the evil book?

Why not, indeed? In a totalitarian society no difficulty arises—no difficulty, at least, that is due to any clash of principles: the infallibility of the state is unquestioned and its authority is paramount; every action of the individual is the direct concern of society, there is no such thing as 'private' conduct; no special value is accorded to personal freedom, no sovereignty is allowed to the claims of art; the only problem for the legislator is to formulate and enforce the necessary restrictive regulations—he is concerned only with the methods, not with the limits, of control. Nor would there be any clash of principles in an entirely anarchical society: each of its members would enjoy, in a measure determined simply by matching his own strength with that of others, the chance-freedom of the free-for-all.

It is where there is an organized society, but a society that recognizes a special value in the full development of the potentialities of the individual, that the legislator is faced by a clash of principles and the citizen becomes conscious of a tension between two pressures, the pressure exerted by the idea of the intrinsic value of personal freedom and the pressure of restrictive regulations designed to secure the general good.

The more highly civilized the society, the greater the likelihood of

[194]

such tension in the individual, for it is a mark of the civilized community that it should set a high value on personal liberty and at the same time—to use words paraphrased from Acton by Lord Radcliffe —'perceive the benefit of compulsory obligations which at a lower stage would be thought unbearable'.

In Britain there has always been, as Lord Radcliffe puts it, 'a special tenderness of sentiment' towards the ideas of liberty and freedom, and above all towards freedom of speech and of the printed word. So strong, indeed, is our feeling for freedom of speech that we are inclined to exaggerate the potency of truth in order to justify the claim that all may speak falsehood if they wish. So we adopt as watchwords, and even accept as platitudes, utterances that are rather aspirations than statements of fact; *Magna est veritas* (we say) *et praevalebit*; 'Let her and falsehood grapple: who ever knew truth put to the worse in a free and open encounter?'

The rhetorical question is justified, no doubt, if a 'free and open encounter' means an encounter in the realm of pure ratiocination; it might be justified even in this workaday world if truth were given the whole length of the future in which to vindicate itself. But if the contest is not between arguments but between ideals of conduct, if the arena is not the debating society but the world we live in, and if we look for a victory in the encounter within a measurable period of time, then there is no justification in fact for the implied assertion from which the rhetoric draws its force. Truth and decency are among the first casualties on too many battlefields, in peace as in war. 'For my part,' says Lord Radcliffe, 'I doubt if men are going to be persuaded to one course or the other by this assertion of an undemonstrable hypothesis which seems again and again to be contradicted by experience.'

In Milton's day, however, and even in the day of Mill, the contest was largely a contest between doctrines, between orthodoxy and heterodoxy; the powerful engines of distortion and suppression that we know today had not been dreamed of; and the plea for unlicensed printing was little more than a blow struck for free expression of opinion in the pamphlet warfare of the time. That battle was duly won; the censor was banished; and since the beginning of the

N*   [195]

eighteenth century the control of the printing press has been in the hands not of the executive but of the legislature and the judiciary, and the limits within which we can say, write, print and (above all) read what we please are prescribed by law and made effective by the courts. Plays and films, it is true, are subject, for special reasons, to pre-censorship; but if we feel inclined to complain of this small inroad on our liberties, we can at least console ourselves, with Sir Charles Snow, by a glance at countries where the stage, the cinema, the novel and the newspaper are all subject to the same iron discipline from above. A British censor's job is a sinecure compared with that of his Vatican counterpart, and he cuts the figure of a feeble amateur by the side of the ruthless professionals in the Kremlin.

In England today we are little concerned with the censorship as a security service for church or state. 'Time and the consolidation of our society,' says Lord Radcliffe, 'have eroded the offence of criminal libel either for seditious or for heretical or blasphemous writings. The nineteenth century saw the end of such publications as effective constituents of crime.' If those offences remain on the Statute Book, it is a reminder of the days of Henry Hunt and Horne Tooke, when the bulwarks of the state needed the buttressing of the criminal code and when religion was, in a very practical sense, 'by law established'. Obscene libel, on the other hand, is by no means a dead letter in the Statute Book, and to conspire to publish such a libel is (according to the recent decision of the House of Lords in *Reg.* v. *Shaw*, the *Ladies' Directory* case) an offence at Common Law.

What, then, is an 'obscene libel'? Under the Jenkins Act—and this has always been the essence of the offence—it is something that has a tendency to 'deprave and corrupt', that is (if the words of the Statute are to be given their dictionary meaning) to make people worse people than they were before they read it.

There are those who would confront the law of obscene libel, so defined, with a challenge on the very threshold: to talk of a person's being 'depraved' by books or pictures is, they say, to disregard the lessons not only of psychology but of everyday life: toy soldiers do not turn children into militarists; licentious novels do not turn grown men into *roués*; every man has within him a set of innate tendencies and potentialities which may be said to constitute his 'moral nature' and which cannot be altered—though of course his conduct may be influenced and his habits moulded—by what he hears or sees. Therefore, it is said, if you prosecute a book or a film on the ground that it 'makes people worse' (and, presumably, if you extol it on the ground that it makes them better) you prove yourself to be the victim of an old-fashioned misconception of how human nature works.

Whether that challenge is well or ill founded, it should be directed, one may suggest, to the wording rather than to the substance of the law. The evanescent distinction between what we are and what we do is not one that the legislator need be troubled with; if conduct of a particular kind is a proper concern of the criminal law, a publication that encourages and facilitates it is not the less objectionable, surely, because it cannot be said, strictly, to alter the natures of those whose behaviour it influences. For the compiler of a criminal code, it is what people do that matters, not what they are. And this, it seems, is recognized by the doctrine of obscene libel at Common Law—or how could the *Ladies' Directory* have come within its scope? The real ground for holding that that publication was a public mischief was surely not that it corrupted or depraved the natures of the pleasure-seekers for whom it catered; all it did was to make it easier for them to find what they were looking for. If it 'corrupted public morals' it was not because it corrupted individuals, but because by facilitating fornication it tended to lower the average standard of moral conduct in the community. Perhaps the Jenkins Act (under which also, incidentally, the *Ladies' Directory* was condemned) should be reworded so as to fall into line with this interpretation of the Common Law, and the statutory definition of obscene libel amended so as to include expressly publications that tend to facilitate or encourage the commission of immoral acts.

But is the definition, even if so amended, satisfactory? 'Immoral acts' and 'corruption' are words with a wide connotation, and the law specifies no particular kind or kinds of depravation as an essential element in the offence: prima facie any published matter that tends to make the citizen in any respect a less moral person is an 'obscene libel'. In practice, it is true, the authorities have recognized what Lord Radcliffe calls 'a submerged equation between moral and sexual conduct', and have administered the law as if it were intended to operate only within the sphere of sex, restricting, in effect, the statutory definition of 'obscene' to its dictionary meaning of impure or lewd. Why, one wonders, has this practical limitation been imposed?

If one asks the jurist what is the justification for this particular interference by the state in the field of morals, a sad confusion is revealed. When, for instance, in *Reg.* v. *Shaw* the Law Lords gave their reasons for holding that a conspiracy to publish an obscene libel was a 'public mischief', Lord Simonds referred to 'the supreme and fundamental purpose of the law, to conserve not only safety and order but also the moral welfare of the state', and went on to say that it mattered little what label was given to the offending act—'an affront to public decency, a corruption of public morals, the creation of a public mischief, the undermining of moral conduct'.

Little though it may matter what label is given to the offending act, it matters much what it is that makes the act 'offending'. An act may, surely, 'affront public decency' without 'undermining moral conduct'; an act may certainly undermine moral conduct without affronting public decency. Does the law of obscene libel, as Lord Simonds seems to suggest, strike equally at both of these? Taken literally—as we have observed—the law would proscribe publications that tend to immorality of any kind. But no one supposes that it should or could be invoked in every sector of the field of morals, and that all books that tend towards immorality should be suppressed on the ground that it is the function of the criminal law to exercise a general superintendence over the morals of the individual. And few would maintain that pornographic works call for suppression, like seditious works, on the ground that they constitute a danger to the framework of society. If that were a reason for suppressing 'obscene libels', the most proper target for prosecution would be, as Lord Radcliffe observes, 'the writer of great literary skill who is impelled by profound sincerity of purpose', for he can do far more, with a sermon or a satire, to undermine the basis on which morality reposes than any cheap pornographer.

The Censor as Aedile

No; one must look elsewhere for the feeling that impels and the motive that justifies prosecutions for publication of an obscene libel. Is it not at least as much the desire to protect members of the public from being disgusted or shocked as it is the desire to protect them from being corrupted or depraved? Is not this the explanation of the 'submerged equation' between sex and morals, and the reason why the pornographic novelette is subjected to prosecution as an obscene libel and not the free-thinking, anti-social tract? In short, is not the real reason for prosecuting an indecent book the fact that it is indecent?

Whether or not this is the 'real' or the only reason, is it not a sufficient one? In order to justify proceeding on this ground against pornography there is no need to invest the criminal law with the dubious character of protector of morals; such prosecutions are a proper exercise of its undisputed function as the preserver of social decency. The law of obscene libel has its place, surely, in the department of the law that forbids 'soliciting' and indecent exposure; it is, to adopt a phrase of Lord Radcliffe's, concerned with 'the old aedile business of keeping the roads clean and the air sweet'.

The notion of decency has not, perhaps, received all the attention it deserves from those who are interested in the relation between law and life. When we are 'shocked' or 'disgusted' by an outrage upon decency, is it our moral or our aesthetic sense that is offended? Or is it some special, intermediate, strand in our sensibility? Why are we shocked more easily by pictures than by descriptions? And why do some things (but not others) shock us only if they are done in public? Our feeling is irrational, no doubt; it has to do with 'taboos'. But is 'culture' a process that consists simply of the shedding of taboos, of ridding ourselves of 'shames' that are not based entirely upon reason? Is it not possible to trace a relationship between the sense of decency in a community and its stage of development as a civilized society? Here is a fruitful field of inquiry for the psychologist, the sociologist, and the anthropologist; and the findings of students in those fields ought, no doubt, to be taken into account by the legislator. Whatever might be the results of such inquiries, in this country the state already recognizes this feeling in its citizens and gives expression to it by forbidding, in appropriate cases, conduct that offends the sense of decency currently prevailing.

'In appropriate cases'—the phrase may seem to beg a large question, but it is surely undeniable that while, on the one hand, the law ought not to convert a mere breach of taste into a criminal offence, one of its functions is to protect the citizen against the impact of conduct, speech, and written or pictorial matter, that outrages the prevailing sense of decency. Copulation or excretion *coram populo*, foul language in the public streets, the display of posters carrying lewd legends or pictures, the hawking of pornographic pamphlets or filthy postcards—such conduct invites by its very indecency the interference of the law; its moral quality is irrelevant. Neither law nor common sense would accept as a defence of the publicly copulating couple the plea that they were man and wife, or that they loved each other very dearly, or that they were making a practical protest against what they sincerely regarded as an out-of-date taboo.

Society's estimate of what is decent and what is not varies, of course, from age to age and from one place to another: in Great Britain a hundred years ago a pamphlet advocating (say) free love or contraception not only would have been deemed immoral by the reading public but would have actually outraged their sense of decency; conduct that would outrage that sense in the average Englishman today may well be considered perfectly proper by African savages or the natives of the South Sea Islands. Decency, like morality itself, is a relative thing; what the law in any society must concern itself with is what shocks here and now; in this respect as in others it must (in Lord Simonds's phrase) 'be related to the changing standards of life' and it is the function of judges and juries, and where necessary of the legislature, to maintain this relation. It is their function also to lay down a standard: it would be neither practicable nor consonant with popular feeling to prosecute conduct that was merely indelicate or mildly disgusting; the law, perforce, takes cognizance not of the peccadillo but of the outrage. Theoretically, perhaps, the legislature should itself prescribe the standard, but that is not the way with our law, and we leave it to the man in the street to determine in the jury-box, under judicial guidance, the point at which the indecent becomes so intolerable that it justifies the interference of the police.

Judges, when directing the jury on this matter, often tell them that they should adopt the standards of a grown man, and not the standards of an inexperienced child. Nowhere is this admonition more desirable than where propriety is in question, for if the standard in such cases were to be set in the nursery, no prosecution for indecency would ever be launched, or would survive a moment if it were. In childhood, innocence and shamelessness go hand in hand; children have no notion of what is shocking and what is not; a sense of propriety is the cultured flower of experience, of society, of civilization. It was not, we may be sure, till after he was taken captive that Caspar Hauser learnt to blush. If then civilization consists as well in the acquisition as in the shedding of taboos, it would seem that a society's sense of decency is something not to be violated rudely, even in the name of 'progress'; we must not, in Burke's phrase, 'subtilize ourselves into savages'; indeed, it is as much the duty of the state— remembering always that 'the here and now' is something neither simple nor static, and making due allowance for gradual shifts and changes in society's ways of thinking and feeling—to keep its citizens shockable as it is its duty to keep them from being shocked.

But, it may be said, our laws against indecency cannot be explained simply by reference to the functions of the aedile; they do not stop short at the inhibition of public conduct; they go further than is required for the protection of the innocent passer-by. 'Strip-tease', for instance, according to the most recent judicial definition of a 'disorderly house' (*Reg.* v. *Quinn*), may amount to an offence at Common Law even if the performance takes place on private premises (provided they are a place of common resort), and it is an offence to publish an obscene libel even if it is supplied only to appreciative customers. In both types of case, as was made plain in *Reg.* v. *Quinn*, a prosecution may be justified on the ground either of an outrage against decency or of a tendency to corrupt.

We have already suggested a doubt whether indecent books or performances in fact either alter people's natures for the worse or even stimulate them to immoral behaviour—may they not rather serve as media of sublimation?—and, even if they do 'put ideas into people's heads', many would deny the censor's right to prohibit them simply in the interests of morality. It was with such objections in mind that we suggested that 'tendency to corrupt' did not offer as satisfactory ground for suppression as 'affront to public decency'. But how, it may be asked, can public decency be affronted by performance in a private place? It is at least a possible answer that the knowledge that such performances are permitted offends against the public's notion of what is decent, and that the law forbidding them gives expression to a feeling analogous to that which insists that certain practices—cannibalism, for instance, necrophily, cruelty to animals, and unnatural vice—are so repugnant to the sensibilities of the Englishman of today that, apart from any consideration of morality or social utility, they should not be permitted in this country in private any more than they are in public.

Perhaps the functions of the aedile merge here in those of the censor—even of the *censor morum*—for there is a depravation that coarsens as well as a depravation that corrupts, and the law might well further justify its interference with such private exhibitions ('We guarantee to members and their guests the spiciest evening of their lives' said the brochure in Quinn's case) not on the questionable ground that they stimulate spectators to indulge in vicious practices, nor on the irrefutable ground that they afford them a degraded pleasure, but because they tend to deaden their sense of what is decent and what is not, and so to lower the standard by which public decency itself is measured.

There is no need, however, to explore the difficulties concerning the law and private conduct, if we are considering a work that has been actually published—that is, made generally available so that it is liable to fall into the hands of all and sundry.

Where circulation is effectively limited by the expense of the production or because the text is veiled in the obscurity of a learned language, doubtless no harm is done; but to offer the offending work to the public at a penny or sixpence or three-and-sixpence a copy is clearly just as bad, from the point of view of social decency, as it would be to give it away. It is no answer to say *caveat emptor*; for the thing will get about, it will lie around; innocent persons other than the purchaser will read it, with the risk of finding it either repellent or attractive, of being either shocked or 'corrupted'—at least in the sense of becoming more difficult to shock.

That leads us to the *cause célèbre* of Lady Chatterley. The Director of Public Prosecutions decided to proceed against the book only under the Jenkins Act, and since that Act makes 'corruption' the essential element in obscenity, the attack in Court was based not upon its intrinsic impropriety but upon its possible effect upon the morals of its readers. But might not the publishers have been proceeded against at the same time under the Common Law, as were the publishers of the *Ladies' Directory*, on the grounds of public mischief? In such proceedings the statutory provisions that the work must be judged 'as a whole', and weight given to 'the interests of literature', would not have applied, and even if the jury had been allowed to take such factors into account their attention might have been focused upon the question of the sheer indecency of the book.

Judged by standards of today, without 'Victorian' squeamishness or prudery, can it be doubted that it must at least by ordinarily accepted standards, be deemed indecent? Would not the ordinary reader be not only shocked by the 'unmentionable' words with which the book is sprinkled but disgusted by the profuse descriptions of male and female *pudenda*; by the allusions to the two 'entrances', and to 'love all ends on', that betray so clearly an anal obsession in the author; and by the vivid word-pictures of so many varieties, natural and unnatural, of the sexual act?

There have been writers who could subdue such words and themes so completely to their artistic purpose that those who are capable of appreciating that purpose to the full simply do not begin to be shocked or disgusted by them. That is true, for instance, of passages in Lucretius's fourth book, Dryden's translation of which has been said to be the finest description of sexual intercourse in the English language; it is true of some of the frankest lyrics of Yeats's old age, and of his famous poem on Leda and the Swan—an 'unmentionable' theme which Correggio's art has similarly redeemed from any taint of possible obscenity. But such an achievement is rare, and Lawrence certainly did not attain it in *Lady Chatterley's Lover*. As has been pointed out in these columns, a serious purpose runs through the book, and it abounds in wonderful imaginative descriptions of the sensations accompanying the act of sex. But the two elements in the novel do not come together; the evangelist of the phallus, now crude and strident, now tediously discursive, shouts down the literary artist, and the thing does not really come off either as an ethical or social tract or as a work of the creative imagination. Mellors the lecturer who speaks the King's English and Mellors the lover who speaks in dialect remain two men; and the latter does not succeed in making plausible the former's message—'Copulate warm-heartedly and everything will come all right'—by expressing it in forthright Anglo-Saxon. And there will be those to whom the recurrent reference to the 'holiness' of sex, and the sentimentality epitomized in the embarrassing last sentence of the book, render Lawrence's treatment of the theme the less, and not the more, acceptable.

At the Old Bailey, however, the case proceeded along different lines. As the jury were repeatedly reminded, the question was not whether the book offended against decency; the case having been brought under the Act of 1959, the charge was in effect one of 'corruption', and the prosecution's main concern was to show that because the author made use of 'unprintable' words, 'glorified sex', and represented Lady Chatterley as unmindful of her marriage vow, therefore the book condoned adulterous intercourse and tended to encourage sexual promiscuity. The defence maintained that 'taken as a whole' it had no such tendency and that even if it was prima facie 'obscene', it was 'for the public good' (apparently as being 'in the interests of literature') that it should be published. They had no difficulty in convincing the jury that the novel was not simply a piece of 'suggestive' pornography but that Lawrence was a serious and considerable author—and that, apparently, was enough to dispose of the case that had been made against them.

And yet one feels that somehow the real issues had been missed. They might have been brought out if the words 'to outrage public decency' had been inserted (as perhaps they ought to be) before the words about 'corrupting' in the Jenkins Act. An odd situation might then have arisen, the defence invoking, 'for the public good', the book's tendency to eliminate 'out-worn' taboos (Lawrence's express object, as avowed in 'Apropos of *Lady Chatterley's Lover*') and frankly challenging that public sense of decency to maintain which would have been a main object of the prosecution. More, also, might then have been made of the description of the 'night of sensual passion'; where, it would seem, Lawrence fails to live up to his gospel of frank expression and takes refuge in that suggestiveness which his defenders stigmatize as the very hall-mark of pornography.

As it was, not only were the real issues missed but there was much clouding of the issues actually debated. Now that one sees their evidence in the cold print of the Penguin series, the procession of witnesses, who so much impressed both the jury and the public, seem, with hardly an exception, to have been testifying rather to their own broadmindedness and high-mindedness than to the literary merit of the book—or, indeed, any other 'object of public concern' about which they might have been called to testify as experts. Much of the evidence, skilfully elicited by their counsel, was simply an expression of their opinions on the question that the jury was being asked to answer, and much of it, on paper, looks pathetic or ridiculous: a Bishop, for instance, stated his view that the book was one that 'Christians ought to read'; a Director of Religious Education informed the Court that the word 'phallic' had been 'baptized by Christians and made into a sacred word'; a girl of twenty-one (who, we are told by Mr. Rolph, 'made a deep impression on the Court') declared that 'the (sexual) relationship was made a very, very serious, important and valuable one, which [*sic*] I think I have very rarely read in any other novel'. Had she really one wonders—and had the Bishop—understood the possible import of the description on page 258 of the 'night of sensual passion'?

One suspects that the jury, even after the Judge's balanced summing-up, were overwhelmed by the fervour and sincerity—and perhaps by the number and respectability—of the witnesses rather than convinced by their evidence on the one point on which it was admissible. Indeed, the jury may have been so much impressed by the evidence on the point on which it was not admissible—whether the book tended to corrupt and to deprave—that they never had to face the difficult task of weighing its 'obscenity' against 'the interests' (whatever they may be) of 'literature' (whatever the legislature may have meant by that). The form of the verdict prevents us from knowing whether they decided that the book was not 'obscene' or that, though 'obscene', it was to be saved on literary ('or other') grounds.

As for that factor of literary merit, the witnesses indulged, to put it mildly, in excessive panegyric, and it is ironical that a work that was applauded at the trial as 'a very great book' should, since the trial, have been very generally defended on the ground that it is so boring that its publication cannot, after all, do anybody any harm.

Mr. Rolph's vivid report of the trial does not, of course, pretend to impartiality; he has an eye on the gallery, and he makes no attempt to conceal his pleasure when he thinks a *gaffe* has been committed by the prosecution or a point scored by the defence; and his pages are punctuated by knowing nudges in his readers' ribs. When we turn to the Rede Lecture, we are moving on another plane. Lord Radcliffe does not linger in the police-court or the Old Bailey; he views the issues in a longer perspective. He looks deep and sees clearly, and he presents his argument in a lucid and telling style, the eloquence of which owes nothing to rhetoric. There is a risk, he says, that if we concern ourselves exclusively with the old complaint about the state's interference with free speech, we may blind ourselves to a more insidious danger: while—to borrow his metaphor—we are defending against the policeman and the censor the old hill fort of liberty of expression, we may be allowing a new and more slippery enemy to stream past and encircle us on the plain.

On the way to his main thesis Lord Radcliffe offers some illuminating observations on the Jenkins Act, calling particular attention to the effect of the new provision—which is but an express statement of the law as already interpreted by several judges—that the alleged libel must be read 'as a whole'. That is a test, as he points out, better designed to discover the intention or purpose of the author than the impact of his work upon most of its readers—few of whom are equipped to appreciate the general effect of a book and many of whom make no attempt to do so. The result of accepting the new criteria will be 'to shift the substance of the criminal offence from the presumed result of what is done to the presumed intention of the person who does it' and to leave liable to conviction only 'the deliberate corrupter without even literary merit'. So that in the end the Act may have the paradoxical effect of turning the aedile back into a *censor morum*, and punishing the offender as much for the evil he intends as for the harm he actually does.

The case of *Lady Chatterley's Lover*, says Lord Radcliffe, 'was not just a nine days' wonder'; but he finds it no easy task to ascertain exactly where its significance lay. He does not see the verdict (like Mr. Rolph and his publishers) as a party triumph, the victory of one 'class and generation' over another; among the least satisfactory of its results, he says, would be 'that it should set off one more cannibal dance round the idea of authority'. For him its significance is rather that it may have marked 'a final turning away from the older idea that words can be things dangerous enough in themselves to merit punishment for the man who has let them loose'. Our increasing sophistication in psychology, he says, has taught us not to accept too easily 'a settled working relationship between stimuli and responses in the matter of words', and he doubts whether, as time goes on, men 'will trouble themselves much about the emotive power of this expression or that, or ... even perceive the old magical association between words and actions'.

It is true, certainly, that psychology has taught us to re-examine links in the causal chain of human behaviour, and we have learnt to revise our views about personal responsibility, with consequences for the law, particularly in relation to punishment. But a long time surely must elapse before either the civil or the criminal law abandons the hypothesis—so necessary for the conduct of day-to-day life among our fellow men—that we can influence people for their good or ill by what we say to them, and before it relieves us from responsibility, for what, rightly or wrongly, we regard as the 'consequences' of our words. Still, the area covered effectively by the law that makes a crime of 'libel' has shrunk progressively, and it may well be that obscene libel will, in time, go the way of its counterparts in the field of blasphemy and sedition.

In the meantime, Lord Radcliffe has a warning to convey, and it is to this warning that he devotes his main energies in this lecture. To-day, the public to which information and entertainment are pur-veyed is increasing even as the number of bodies and individuals who control the organs of distribution is diminishing, so that fewer and fewer persons decide in effect what larger and larger masses shall hear and see and read. The motives of the controllers are various, and may be mixed; they do not see their control as a censorship, and do not exercise it in the name or the interests of government, of party, of authority; but they employ criteria that take little account of ethical and artistic considerations, and their dominating aim is the dangerously innocent one of giving the largest amount of satisfac-tion to the largest possible number of people. Writers, thinkers, artists, who do not conform to the general average of taste and opinion—or, worse still, to an average imputed to the public by persons who have little discrimination themselves and small power to judge of it in others—are in danger of being effectively and com-pletely muzzled by the operation of contemporary methods of dis-seminating words, ideas, and images. The 'engines of production' are 'huge and monopolistic', their standards are 'uniform' and 'repetitive', and they lack conviction. 'The organizational pattern', says Lord Radcliffe, 'is discouraging. The censors will be very powerful and they will not even be identified as censors.' The outlook is not a bright one for those who care for quality or are interested in the independent flowering of thought or of the arts.

Wherein lies a hope for those who dread an almost total degrada-tion of our culture? Beyond faith in a 'fecundity of ideas' and in a self-reliance on the part of the educated man which he believes to be a phenomenon of the present scientific age, Lord Radcliffe has no positive prescription to offer. But he has turned a searchlight on the enemy, and his lecture gives a clear warning that that enemy cannot be defeated by using the weapons, or by repeating the war-cries, of a bygone age.

The Censor as Aedile

NOTE

'The Censor as Aedile' appeared in *The Times Literary Supplement* for 4 August 1961 as a review of Lord Radcliffe's Rede Lecture, *Censors*, and of the Penguin 'Transcript' of the proceedings in the case *Regina* v. *Penguin Books Limited*. The interpretation of certain passages in *Lady Chatterley's Lover* suggested in my review (see pp. 203, 205 above) was alluded to as being probably correct by Mr. Andrew Shonfield in a Note, 'Lawrence's Other Censor', in *Encounter* for September 1961, and its correctness was assumed by Professor G. Wilson Knight in an article, 'Lawrence, Joyce and Powys', in *Essays in Criticism* for October 1961. I myself sought to justify that interpretation by a closely-reasoned analysis of the relevant contexts in an essay, 'Regina v. Penguin Books Limited. An Undisclosed Element in the Case', in *Encounter* for February 1962. My essay provoked a large volume of criticism, much of it most intemperate, on the ground that my interpretation was simply wrong (this was, I gather, the attitude that would have been adopted by the defence had the issue been raised at the trial) and on the ground that it was so obviously right that the proof of it contained in my article was quite superfluous. I replied to my critics in a further essay, 'Afterthoughts on Regina v. Penguin Books', in *Encounter* for June 1962. The point at issue is so vital for a true assessment of Lawrence's 'sexual ethic' (cf. the chapter on *Lady Chatterley's Lover* in Professor Elisea Vivas's *D. H. Lawrence: the Failure and Triumph of Art*) that I was tempted, repugnant though the subject is to many readers, to reprint my essays in the present volume; but their tone and treatment would have rendered them, I think, out of key with the rest of its contents, and I have therefore not included them.